HANDLING BEREAVEMENT
MAKING ARRANGEMENTS
FOLLOWING DEATH

Penny Freeman

Editor: Roger Sproston

Straightforward Guides
www.straightforwardco.co.uk

Straightforward Guides

© Straightforward Co Ltd 2022

British Library Cataloguing in Publication Data. A catalogue record is available for this book from the British Library.

ISBN

978-1-80236-055-4

Printed and bound by 4edge www.4edge.co.uk

Cover design by BW Studio Derby

Whilst every effort has been taken to ensure that the information contained in this book was accurate at the time of going to print, the publisher and the author cannot accept any liability for any inaccuracies contained within or for changes in legislation since writing the book.

CONTENTS

Introduction

1. Death and the registration of death   **17**

Laying out a body   17

Police involvement   18

Certificate of cause of death   19

The coroner   19

Registration of death   22

Registrars' requirements   23

The Presumption of Death Act 2013   26

Registering a stillbirth   26

Death in a hospital   29

Carrying out a post-mortem in hospital   31

The donations of organs for transplantation   31

Organs that can be transplanted   35

The National Health Service Organ

Donor Register   38

Donation of a body for medical causes   38

Donation of the brain for medical research   39

Registration in Scotland   39

Death certificates   42

Death abroad   42

2. Steps after registration — 49

3. Taking decisions about a funeral — 53

Costs of a funeral — 56

Funeral Plans and other financial plans — 56

Associated costs — 66

Obtaining help with funeral costs — 67

4.The Burial-Main Points — 71

The burial — 71

Burial in cemeteries — 72

Types of grave — 74

Other burial places — 75

Cremation — 75

Fees for cremation — 77

Services in a crematorium — 78

Cremations and memorials — 78

Remains — 79

5. Events Before a Funeral — 83

Embalming a body — 84

The final arrangements before a funeral — 85

Non-Church of England funerals — 85

Non-religious services — 86

The funeral — 87

The burial — 88

Cremation   89
Burial in Scotland   90
Arranging a funeral without a funeral director   90
Green Funerals   92
Real Green Funerals   92
The Natural Death Centre   94

6. Different funerals   **95**
Muslim funerals   95
Hindu funerals   96
Sikh funerals   97
Buddhist funerals   97
Jewish funerals   100
Cult funerals   101

7. After a funeral is over   **103**
Traditional funerals   103
Memorials   104
After cremation   104
Charitable donations   106

8. Applying for probate in England and Wales,
   Scotland and Northern Ireland.
When probate is not needed   107
Who can apply   107
If there's a will   108

If the person did not leave a will   108
Work out who inherits   109
If you're an executor   109
If there's more than one executor   110
If you do not want to or cannot be an executor 110
Before you apply   111
Probate application fees   111
Get help and advice   111
Apply for probate online   111
Apply for probate by post   112
If the will has been changed or damaged   114
After you've applied   114
Probate in Scotland   114
Applying for probate in Northern Ireland   118

9. The intervention of the courts   123
Introduction   123
Who can apply for an order?   123
When to apply for an order   124
Grounds for making a claim   124
Orders the court can make   125
Factors the court must consider   126
The procedure   128
Legal costs   130

10. Welfare benefits after bereavement   **131**

Bereavement benefits if you were married or in   131
a civil partnership

Bereavement Support Payment   131

How much is Bereavement Support Payment?   132

How do I claim Bereavement Support Payment?   133

Bereavement benefits if you were living together   133

How to claim benefits if you're on a low income   134

Funeral Payment   134

How much you will get   135

How your bereavement benefits affect other
benefits   135

Benefits calculators   136

Tax and National Insurance   136

Financial help death in the armed forces   141

Tell Us Once Service   141

Update Property records   147

Useful addresses

Index

****

Introduction

Death is an unpleasant reality and one that many people avoid thinking about. However, on the death of a person who is close there are very necessary actions that need to be taken. This book, updated to 2022, and which now includes probate in Scotland and Northern Ireland, is an attempt to enlighten the reader as to the practical steps that need to be taken after the death of a person. Each step is outlined along with the role of the funeral director and the role of the church and crematoria after death.

The Coronavirus and the effect on funerals

The coronavirus pandemic has obviously influenced funerals and those who attend funerals. The government issued guidance on funerals and attendance at funerals on their website:

www.gov.uk/government/publications/covid-19-guidance-for-managing-a-funeral-during-the-coronavirus-pandemic.

Although restrictions have now been relaxed, basically, safety first in all aspects of organising and carrying out a funeral is still the main underlying message!

In the book, the role of the coroner is outlined and also the doctor, registrar, clergymen and cemetery and crematorium officials. This book does not dwell in depth on bereavement counselling, as this is a separate area and warrants a book on its own. It does, however, outline the process of grief and discuss aspects of this and offers advice in a limited way. The book is very much a practical guide and has been written in the hope that people may benefit from it at this difficult time.

There is a section on non-Christian burial in the recognition that the United Kingdom is a diverse multi-racial society and different traditions apply to different cultures. There is also a section on wills and probate, as dealing with an estate after death can be very complex and time consuming, particularly if there is no will. Finally, there is a list of useful addresses at the end of the book. Before we look at the practical side of handling death, we will look at bereavement generally.

Bereavement generally

Bereavement affects people in different ways. There's no right or wrong way to feel. You might feel a lot of emotions at once, or feel you're having a good day, then you wake up and feel worse again. Experts generally accept that there are four stages of bereavement:

- accepting that your loss is real
- experiencing the pain of grief
- adjusting to life without the person who has died
- putting less emotional energy into grieving and putting it into something new (in other words, moving on)

You'll probably go through all these stages, but you won't necessarily move smoothly from one to the next. Your grief might feel chaotic and out of control, but these feelings will eventually become less intense. Give yourself time, as they will pass. You might feel:

- shock and numbness (this is usually the first reaction to the death, and people often speak of being in a daze)
- overwhelming sadness, with lots of crying
- tiredness or exhaustion
- anger, for example towards the person who died, their illness or God
- guilt, for example guilt about feeling angry, about something you said or didn't say, or about not being able to stop your loved one dying

These feelings are all perfectly normal. Lots of people feel guilty about their anger, but it's natural to be angry and to question why.

The GOV.UK website has information on what to do after someone dies, such as registering the death and planning a funeral. One particularly important service that we will be referring to in detail in chapter 10 is the Tell us Once service that enables people to input details relating to benefits, passport, driving licence etc and enables the bereaved party to deal with all government departments at once. This is in recognition of the fact that the last thing people want, in such a difficult time, is for government departments breathing down their necks. For more information, go to

https://www.gov.uk/.../organisations-you-need-to-contact-and-tell-us-once

Coping with grief

Talking and sharing your feelings with someone can help. Don't go through this alone. For some people, relying on family and friends is the best way to cope. But if you don't feel you can talk to them much (perhaps you aren't close, or they're grieving too), you can contact local bereavement services through your GP, local hospice, or the National Cruse helpline on 0808 808 1677.

A bereavement counsellor can give you time and space to talk about your feelings, including the person who has died, your relationship, family, work, fears, and the future. You can have access to a bereavement counsellor at any time, even if the person you lost died a long time ago.

Don't be afraid to talk about the person who has died. People in your life might not mention their name because they don't want to upset you. But if you feel you can't talk to them, it can make you feel isolated.

If you need help to move on

Each bereavement is unique, and you can't tell how long it will last. In general, the death and the person might not constantly be at the forefront of your mind after around 18 months. This period may be shorter or longer for some people, which is normal.

Your GP or a bereavement counsellor can help if you feel that you're not coping. Some people also get support from a religious minister.

You might need help if:

- you can't get out of bed
- you neglect yourself or your family, for example you don't eat properly
- you feel you can't go on without the person you've lost
- the emotion is so intense it's affecting the rest of your life, for example you can't face going to work or you're taking your anger out on someone else

13

These feelings are normal if they don't last for a long time. The time to get help depends on the person, if these things last for a period that you feel is too long, or your family say they're worried, that's the time to seek help. Your GP can refer you, and they can monitor your general health.

Some people turn to alcohol or drugs during difficult times. Get help cutting down on alcohol, or see the Frank website www.talktofrank.com for information on drugs.

The Death Café Movement

Inspired by the work of Bernard Crettaz, a Swiss Sociologist, John Underwood, the Founder of the Death Café Movement created the first Temporary Death Café in 2011 in the basement of his home in London. The movement quickly spread to over 4000 temporary Cafes throughout the world.

The idea is that people can discuss all aspects of death, from the practical aspects i.e., what to do when someone dies and also sharing tales of bereavement, such as personal experiences and also one's own view of death. The overall aim is to allow people to be open about death and all that surrounds it.

To find out more and locate a Death Café near to you go to deathcafe.com

Pre-bereavement care

If someone has an incurable illness, they and their loved ones can prepare for bereavement. Bereavement counsellors offer pre-bereavement care, helping patients and their family cope with their feelings. This can be especially important for children, children's stress levels are at their highest before their family member dies, so support during this time is important.

You can find out more about children and bereavement from the Childhood Bereavement Network. In the next chapter, we will look at the first steps involved in handling a death, which is the registration of death.

****

Ch.1

Death and the Registration of Death

If you suspect a person is dead, the first thing that you should do is to tell a doctor. There may be some doubt as to whether the person has died. In all cases, call a doctor or phone the ambulance service. Ask whether the doctor is going to attend. If the death of a person has been expected, then it may not be immediately necessary for a doctor to attend late at night, the next morning will do.

If the doctor does not intend to come, for reasons made very clear, remove the body. If a decision has been made that the funeral will be a cremation, the doctor will need to know as special papers will need to be drawn up which will involve an inspection, separately, by two doctors. If you intend to keep a body at home prior to such an inspection, which can be carried out in a funeral parlour, then it will be necessary to keep the room at a cool temperature.

Laying out a body

This is the first stage in preparing a body for burial or cremation. If carried out by a funeral director it is termed last offices, the "first office", denoting either the first or last contact. The body is washed and tidied up, eyelids closed, and jaw closed. Hair is tidied, arms and legs and hair usually grows for some time after a death so therefore will need shaving. If a funeral director is laying out a body, then gown or everyday clothes will be applied.

Although laying out and general preparation can be carried out at home, and a funeral director can also provide a service in the home, it is usual to allow the body to be taken away to a funeral parlour. An occurrence after death is Rigor Mortis, which is a stiffening of the muscles. This normally begins six hours after death and takes effect all over the body within 24 hours, after which it usually begins to wear off. In addition, about half an hour after death parts of the dead persons skin will begin to show dark patches. This activity is called Hypostasis and is due to settlement of the blood in the body due to gravity.

Police involvement

In certain circumstances it may be necessary to call the police if a person's death is not due to natural circumstances. It could be that a death is the result of murder or other suspicious circumstance. It is very important not to touch anything in the room as you may disturb vital evidence. The police will take statements from anyone who was with the person before death. There may at times be difficulty in identifying a dead body and the police have a specific procedure in this case.

Certificate of cause of death

In the United Kingdom, every death must be recorded in the local registrar's office within five days. The Registrar will always require a certificate as to the cause of death. If the cause of death is known then the doctor attending on death will provide the certificate, which states the cause, when last seen alive and whether any doctor has seen the body since death occurred. This certificate will be given to the family. No charge is usually made. If the doctor concerned is uncertain about the cause of death or has not seen the body for 14 days after death, then a certificate cannot be issued, and the coroner's office is informed. The body is taken to the coroner's mortuary and a post-mortem may or may not be carried out.

The coroner

A Coroner is a qualified doctor or solicitor and is paid by the local authority. The coroner is independent of both local and central government and is responsible only to the Crown. The coroner is assisted by the coroner's officer, usually a police officer. The coroner's office has contact with the public. It has to be said that the functions of the coroner have, like all other areas of life, been affected by the pandemic.

When a death occurs which is not due to natural causes it must be reported to the coroner. If the deceased died of natural causes but was not seen by a doctor for a significant time before death or after death, then the coroner must be reported to. The deceased person's doctor will be contacted, and cause of death and circumstances ascertained. If satisfied the coroner will cease involvement and issue a certificate and the family can then register the death normally.

In any cases where the doctor is uncertain as to the cause of the death then the coroner must be notified. Death resulting from industrial disease, which has given rise to compensation, must be reported to the coroner. In addition, death arising from military service must be reported, in some but not all cases. Other circumstances in which death has arisen which must be reported are:

- If the death was suspicious
- Was sudden or unexplained
- Due to neglect, i.e., poisoning, drugs etc
- Caused directly or indirectly by accident
- Suicide
- In prison or police custody

Another situation is during surgery or before recovering from the effects of anaesthetic. When a death is reported to a coroner, and an investigation is decided upon then a death cannot be registered until enquiries are complete. There will usually be a post-mortem. If death is shown to be from natural causes, then the family will be notified, and the death can be registered normally.

The family of the deceased do not have to be consulted or asked about carrying out a post- mortem. If the law requires it, then the coroner must proceed. However, if a family or individual objects they can register that objection with the coroner who must listen and give reasons for a post-mortem. If there are still objections there is the right of appeal to the High Court. This will delay disposal of the body. The coroner has no duty to inform the next of kin about findings of a post-mortem. After the post-mortem, and a coroner's report made to the relevant authorities, the body becomes the responsibility of the family.

The coroner is obliged to hold an inquest into every violent and unnatural death and death whilst in prison. The inquest is open to the public and can take the form of a trial, with witnesses called. The office of the coroner is a powerful office, and the intention is to ensure that death was natural and not due to violent or other unnatural means. After the inquest is over then the death can be registered in the normal way.

Information concerning death, including the handing in of a certificate or the informing of the registrar of an extended period without certificate due to post-mortem or other

21

examination, can be given at any registrar's office (In England and Wales). This will then be passed on to the appropriate district or sub office.

Registration of death

As stated, in England, Wales and Northern Ireland a death should be registered within five days of occurrence (8 days in Scotland, to the Procurator Fiscal see below registering a death in Scotland).

Registration can be delayed for up to another nine days if the registrar receives written confirmation that a doctor has signed a medical certificate of cause of death. The medical certificate must be presented at the register office in the sub-district where the death occurred. The person registering the death must decide how many copies of the death certificate is needed and pay for them at the office. Payment can be by cheque, or credit card if ordering online or by telephone. The registration is free. Any certified copies of death certificates will be £11 (2022) in England and Wales at the time of registration.

After registration, for up to one month, the cost of a copy certificate will be £11. If you require a copy certificate urgently, you may wish to use the Priority Service. The cost for this service is £35. You can check current fees at www.gov.uk/order-copy-birth-death-marriage-certificate.

There is a different process in Scotland and Northern Ireland, information of which can also be obtained from the website. Another very good and clear website is: www.which.co.uk/later-life-care/end-of-life/what-to-do-when-someone-dies/registering-a-death-

If the death certificate is to be sent to someone else, then the details must be given to the registrar. It is possible at this stage for what is known as the "Green certificate" authorising burial or cremation to be sent to the funeral director carrying out the funeral arrangements.

Names addresses and phone numbers of local registrars can be found in doctors' surgeries, libraries etc.

Registrar's requirements

Registrar's information is contained on a part of a medical certificate issued by the doctor. This part is entitled "notice to informant" and lists:

- The date and place of death
- The full name, including maiden name if appropriate of the deceased
- Date of birth
- Occupation
- Occupation of the husband if deceased was a married woman or widow
- Address

- Whether deceased was in receipt of pension or allowance from public funds
- If the deceased was married, the date of birth of the surviving partner.

The form also states that the deceased's medical card should be given to the registrar. The other side of this form gives details of who is qualified to inform the registrar of a death. If the death occurs in a house or any other public building, the following can inform a registrar of a death:

- A relative of the deceased who was present at the death
- A relative who was present during the last illness
- A relative of the deceased who was not present at the death or during the last illness but who lives in the district or sub-district where the death occurred
- A person who is not a relative but who was present at the time of death
- The occupier of the building where the death occurred, if aware of the details of death
- Any inmate of the building where the death occurred, if aware of the details of death
- The person causing the disposal of the body, meaning the person accepting responsibility for arranging the

funeral, but not the funeral director, who cannot register the death

The above is in order of preference. If a person has been found dead elsewhere, the following are qualified to register the death:

- Any relative of the dead person able to provide the registrar with the required details
- Any person present at time of death
- The person who found the body
- The person in charge of the body (which will be the police if the body cannot be identified)
- The person accepting responsibility for arranging the funeral

Only a person qualified under the law can inform the registrar of the death. If the registrar considers that the cause of death supplied on the medical certificate is inadequate, or the death should have been reported to the coroner, the registrar must inform the coroner and wait for written authority to proceed before continuing with registration. In cases where a coroner's inquest has been held, the coroner will act as the person informing death.

The Presumption of Death Act 2013

The Presumption of Death Act, 2013, passed after years of campaigning, will allow relatives to apply for a single certificate declaring someone presumed dead, helping them resolve that person's affairs. Its creation follows a campaign by the charity Missing People, and relatives of missing people, including Peter Lawrence, father of missing chef Claudia Lawrence, and Rachel Elias, the sister of Manic Street Preachers guitarist Richey Edwards who went missing in 1995.

Their concerns were raised before the Justice Select Committee and the All-Party Parliamentary Group for Runaway and Missing Children and Adults, and the new law was passed. The new law, based on the Scottish Presumption of Death Act 1977, only allows families to apply for a presumption of death order after seven years.

Campaigners said they will continue to fight for another law on guardianship, allowing families to maintain a missing person's estate during these years by cancelling direct debits, paying off debts, and providing maintenance for dependants.

Registering a stillbirth

A stillbirth should be registered at a register office within 42 days. Sometimes a stillbirth can be registered after 42 days -

the register office can explain when this can happen. You can name the baby in the register.

In Scotland you must register a stillbirth within 21 days. In Northern Ireland you have up to 1 year to register a stillbirth.

Who can register the stillbirth?

- If the baby's parents are married, either the mother or father can register. The mother can sign if:
- the baby's parents are not married
- the father cannot be traced or is unknown
- If both parents want the father's name in the register:
- both parents can sign the register together
- the mother can sign and bring a 'signed declaration' from the father (the register office can explain how to do this).
- If the father registers the stillbirth and the parents are not married, the mother will need to make a 'signed declaration' (the register office can explain how to do this). If the child was conceived as a result of fertility treatment Either of the following can register the stillbirth:
- the mother
- the father if he was married to the mother at the time of treatment

- the second female parent if she was in a civil partnership with the mother at the time of treatment

If neither parent can attend

The following people can register the stillbirth:

- the occupier of the hospital or house where the stillbirth took place
- someone who was present at the stillbirth
- someone who is responsible for the stillborn child
- the person who found the stillborn child, if the date and place of the stillbirth are unknown

What you need to take

You need the medical certificate of stillbirth issued by the doctor or midwife. You can arrange a funeral for your baby.

Financial support and taking time off work

Following a stillbirth, you're normally entitled to:

- Statutory Maternity Pay - if you're employed
- Maternity Allowance - if you're not entitled to Statutory Maternity Pay
- Maternity Leave - if you're employed
- Statutory Paternity Pay - if you're employed
- Paternity Leave - if you're employed

You will be asked for evidence to get financial support. This can be the notification for the registration of a stillbirth from the attending doctor or midwife, or a certificate of stillbirth from the registrar. You will not be able to claim Child Benefit.

Support organisations

The following organisations give support and advice:

Sands www.sands.org.uk 0808 164 3332

Tommy's www.tommys.org 0208 398 3400

A lot of funeral directors will give their services free of charge on such occasions, although there may be a fee for crematoria that is incurred on behalf of clients. Some hospitals offer reverent disposal of stillborn and miscarried children, which often involves a simple ceremony led by a chaplain. In such cases there may be no ashes for subsequent burial or scattering.

Death in a hospital

There is a slight difference to the procedures up to the time of registration if a death is in hospital. The relatives or next of kin are informed of the death by the hospital staff. If death was unexpected, for example, the result of an operation or accident, the coroner will be involved. Usually, all deaths occurring within 24 hours of an operation will be reported to

29

the coroner. The coroner must by law be informed of all deaths under suspicious circumstances, or death due to medical mishap, industrial disease, violence, neglect, abortion, or any kind of poisoning. If the person who died was not already an in-patient in a hospital, then a member of the family may be asked to identify the body.

In cases where the coroner is involved it will not be possible to issue a medical certificate of the cause of death, but in other cases this is usually issued by the hospital doctor and given to the next of kin. If the person died before the hospital doctor had the chance to diagnose the cause, then the deceased patient's own doctor may be sometimes asked to issue the medical certificate. The deceased's possessions will have to be removed from the hospital, with a receipt needing to be signed on removal. If the medical certificate of the cause of death can be signed in the hospital, then relatives will have to decide to remove the body from the hospital mortuary. This will usually be the responsibility of the funeral director.

Most funeral directors operate a 24-hour emergency service. However, there is no need to inform the director of a hospital death until the morning after death. If cremation is involved, the necessary forms will be filled in at the hospital. The body cannot be removed until this is done. There will be a charge for filling in the forms.

Carrying out a post-mortem in a hospital

A hospital will sometimes wish to carry out a post-mortem, not involving the coroner. This cannot be carried out without the permission of the next of kin. In cases where a coroner is involved permission is not required. If a coroner orders a post-mortem then this is legally required and cannot be prevented. Results are not automatically given to relatives and a request for these may have to be made. The procedure for registering a death is the same as for a death outside a hospital. The registration, however, must be within the district where the hospital is situated. Where there are no relatives or others to meet the cost of the funeral then the health authority has the power to do so. There are usually arrangements with local funeral directors to provide a simple funeral for the deceased.

The donation of organs for transplantation

On 20 May 2020, the law around organ donation in England was changed to help save and improve more lives. It is now an op-out system. The opt-out system works on the understanding that all adults agree to become organ donors when they die, unless they have made it known that they do not wish to donate. The opt out system applies to everyone in England, except for those who are part of what are called excluded groups.

Excluded groups are:

- Those under the age of 18
- People who lack the mental capacity to understand the new arrangements and take the necessary action
- Visitors to England, and those not living here voluntarily
- People who have lived in England for less than 12 months before their death

If you have not recorded an organ donation decision and you are not in one of the excluded groups, it will be considered that you agree to donate your organs, when you die. You may hear this system referred to as the opt out system, deemed consent, presumed consent or Max and Keira's Law. You can still choose whether you want to be an organ donor when you die by registering your decision and telling your family. Your faith, beliefs and culture will continue to be respected.

Wales

The legislation for Wales is 'deemed consent'. This means that if you haven't registered an organ and tissue donation decision (opt in or opt out), you will be considered to have no objection to becoming a donor. You can still opt into the register if you want to do so, but it is not required to give consent for donation. You can also nominate up to two representatives to make the decision for you. These could be family members, friends, or other people you trust, such as your faith leader.

Northern Ireland

The current legislation for Northern Ireland is to opt in to organ and tissue donation; you can do this by joining the NHS Organ Donor Register and sharing your decision with your family. You can also record a decision not to be a donor. You can also nominate up to two representatives to make the decision for you. These could be family members, friends, or other people you trust, such as your faith leader.

Following consideration of the issue, in 2020 the health minister said he intends to hold a consultation moving towards introducing a soft opt-out system for organ donation in Northern Ireland. The consultation is expected to begin in the autumn.

In addition, the Northern Ireland Assembly introduced a new statutory requirement for the Department of Health to promote organ donation as a means of increasing the number of organs available for transplantation.

Every five years the department will be required to provide the Northern Ireland Assembly with advice about whether efforts to promote organ donation have been effective, and any recommendations it considers appropriate for amending the law to further promote transplantation.

Organ and tissue donation in Scotland

In July 2019, the Human Tissue (Authorisation) (Scotland) Act 2019 gained Royal Assent. The legislation sets out an opt out system of organ and tissue donation for transplantation. From 26 March 2021 if you die in circumstances where you could become a donor and have not recorded a donation decision, it may be assumed you are willing to donate your organs and tissue for transplantation. This is commonly referred to as an 'opt out' system and will apply to most adult's resident in Scotland.

You still have a choice if you want to be a donor or not when you die, and you do not have to wait until March 2021 to make this decision.

The best way to record your donation decision is by registering either an opt-in or opt-out decision on the NHS Organ Donor Register. If you do not record a decision, it may be assumed that you are willing to become a donor. Your family will always be asked about your latest views on donation, to ensure it would not proceed if this was against your wishes.

Under the new system there will be protections for adults without capacity to understand deemed authorisation, adult's resident in Scotland for less than 12 months and children under the age of 16 will not be subject to deemed authorisation and will only be able to donate if they, or someone on their behalf, explicitly authorises it.

Generally

Organ transplants help to save the lives of several thousand people per year and some thought needs to be given as to the possibility of donating organs from the dead person. Organs must be removed as soon as possible after death to prevent deterioration, which renders them useless. No organ can be removed for transplantation until a person is declared brain dead, known as "stem", death. To determine brain stem death several stringent tests are carried out, the criteria of which are laid down by the Royal College of Surgeons.

A patient must be under 75 years of age for their major organs to be suitable for transplantation. The patient must be HIV negative and free from major infection. He or she must be of a compatible blood group to the planned recipient of the organs.

Organs that can be transplanted

Essentially, the organs intended for transplant must be in good order. For example, the lungs of a heavy smoker would be unsuitable. The following are the most used for transplantation:

Heart

Heart transplants are considered for those patients with severe cardiac failure who are considered unsuitable for heart surgery.

Kidney

Kidneys are viable for around 48 hours following retrieval from the donor.

Liver

Liver transplants are required for patients with congenital malformation of the liver, hepatic failure, chronic liver disease, some cases of cancer and inborn metabolic errors.

Heart and lung

This operation is carried out for people with an advanced primary lung disease, or a condition leading to this, or lung disease arising because of cardiac problems.

The pancreas

Pancreas transplants are used for patients with type 1 diabetes. This operation may be solely a pancreas transplant or can be done together with the kidneys.

Lungs

One or both lungs can be transplanted.

Cornea

Damage to the cornea is a major cause of blindness. Cornea grafting is one major solution to blindness. There is no age limit for corneal donation and corneas can be removed up to 24 hours after the heart has stopped beating. Relatives of patients not dying in a hospital who want to carry out their wishes should first consult the donors GP or the ophthalmic department of the local hospital.

Heart valves

These can be transplanted following removal from a donor up to 72 hours after death. There are other parts of the body, which can be transplanted including the skin, bone, connective tissue, major blood vessels, fettle cells and bone marrow. When deciding whether to donate organs, religious and other cultural considerations will play a significant part. For Christians, organ donation is considered acceptable to Roman Catholics and Protestants. Christian Scientists, on the other hand, object to all forms of transplants. Buddhists do not object neither does the Jewish faith, except for some orthodox Jews. Mormons have no objection neither do Hindu and Sikh. Muslims tend towards prohibition of organ transplants.

The National Health Service Organ Donor Register

This register is a computer data-base set up at the UK Transplant Support Service Authority (UKTSSA). All transplant coordinators have access to the register, and it can be checked each time a donor becomes available. Although relatives of donors are still asked for their permission to donate, the fact that details are on the register and there is a donor card carried, the decision is made easier by inclusion on the register.

Any driving licence issued after 1993 may be marked on the back indicating willingness to donate organs. Anyone wishing to be entered onto the register can do so by post or using a form available from doctor's surgeries, chemists, libraries, and other public places.

Donation of a body for medical uses

Some people wish their body to used for medical education or research after death. If this was the wish of the deceased, then the next of kin or the executor should contact HM Inspector of Anatomy for details of the relevant anatomy school. This should be done immediately after death. Offering a body may not lead to it being accepted due to too many offers or the nature of the death or whether the coroner is involved or how far away the body is.

Donation of the brain for medical research

Brain donation is a separate issue altogether from Organ donation and cannot be included on the NHS register. The Parkinson' Disease Society Brain Research Centre, which is part of the Institute of Neurology at the University College of London must be instructed to the effect that the donor wishes to donate the brain and potential donors must inform the society in advance or leave clear instructions that this should be done in the event of their death.

It will be the responsibility of the medical school to decide and pay for the funeral. The school will decide for a simple funeral unless the relatives indicate otherwise.

More about registration in Scotland

New arrangements for the certification and registration of deaths in Scotland were introduced on 13 May 2015. This included the establishment of an independent review service run by Healthcare Improvement Scotland. Information on all aspects of the Death Certification Review Service is available on the Healthcare Improvement Scotland website. One of the main changes is the establishment of the Death Certification Review Service which is run by Healthcare Improvement Scotland. The review service checks on the accuracy of a sample of Medical Certificates of Cause of Death (MCCDs). An MCCD is the form a doctor completes when someone has died.

39

The Scottish Government booklet "What to do after a death in Scotland" is available on the Scottish Government website www.mygov.scot/register-death-coronavirus.

This gives practical advice for bereaved people and is widely available in registration offices.

There are also instructions on the website on what to do to register a death remotely during the COVID pandemic, as most of the offices have been closed or are still closed.

In Scotland the medical certificate of the cause of death is very similar to that in England. The obligation to give a certificate rests on the doctor who attended the dead person during their last illness. If there was no certificate in attendance, then any doctor can issue a certificate. In most cases the certificate is given to a relative who will then send or give it to the Registrar of Deaths in their area. If a medical certificate of cause of death cannot be given, the registrar can register the death but must report the matter to the Procurator Fiscal.

There are no coroners as such in Scotland and the duties of a coroner are carried out by a Procurator fiscal. This person is a law officer and comes under the jurisdiction of the Lord Advocate. The key functions of the procurator fiscal include responsibility for the investigation of all unexpected deaths including those under suspicious circumstances. If he or she is satisfied with the doctor's medical certificate and any police evidence, then no further action will usually be taken. If there is doubt, then a medical surgeon will be asked to report. In most cases, a post-mortem is not carried out and the doctor certifies the cause of death after an external examination.

In those situations where a post-mortem is deemed necessary then permission is sought from the sheriff. Where there is a possibility of criminal proceedings connected to the death then two surgeons will usually carry out the post-mortem.

Death whilst in legal custody or at work must be the subject of a public enquiry which will take the place of an inquest in England. If the death is by natural causes, then there may not be a public enquiry. A public enquiry is held before the sheriff in the local sheriff court. The procurator fiscal examines the witnesses, but it is the sheriff who determines the cause of death. When the enquiry is completed the procurator fiscal notifies the result of the findings to the registrar general.

If the death has not already been registered, then the registrar general lets the local registrar in the district in which the death occurred know of the death.

In Scotland the law requires that every death must be registered within eight days of death. The person qualified to act as an informant is any relative of the dead person, any person present at the death, the deceased executor or other

41

representative, the occupier of the premises where the death took place, or any person having knowledge of the particulars to be registered.

The death may be registered in the office for the district in which the death occurred or in the office in the district where the deceased had resided before his or her death. The death of anyone visiting Scotland must be registered where the death took place.

Death Certificates

As is the practice in England, the Registrar will issue free of charge a certificate of registration of death which can be used for National Insurance purposes. All other death certificates carry a fee. A list of fees for the various functions carried out by the registrar can be obtained from any registrar's office, as in England.

When someone dies abroad

When someone dies abroad, the death may seem more distressing because of the complications of being away from home and dealing with strangers, but you can get help from the British authorities in the UK and overseas.

If the death has been reported to the British Consulate in the country where the person died, they will ask the UK police to inform the next of kin. If you hear of the death from someone else, for example a tour operator, you should contact the Foreign Commonwealth and Development Office (FCDO) on 020 7008 5000. Consular staff in London will keep in touch with the family and the Consulate abroad until burial or cremation overseas or until the deceased has been brought back to the UK. They will also tell the British Consul of your wishes for the funeral and take details of who will be responsible for paying the costs involved, such as bringing the body back to the UK.

If the person dies while you are abroad with them

The British Consul will support you by offering practical advice and help with funeral arrangements and other formalities such as inquests. If the person died while on a package holiday, the tour operator will be able to contact funeral directors and British Consular staff for you.

Registering the death where the person died

You will need to register the death according to local regulations and get a death certificate.

The local police, British Consul or tour guide can advise you on how to do this. You can also often register the death at the British Consulate as well. You don't have to do this, but if you do you will be given a UK Death Certificate and a record will be kept at the General Registrar's Office 'Overseas' records in the UK. You will also be able to get a copy of the Death certificate later from the General Register Office or from the British Consul in the country concerned. It is not possible to register the death with the British authorities in Australia, Canada, New Zealand, Ireland, South Africa, or Zimbabwe.

Documents that you will need to register the death

When registering the death, you should take information about yourself and the deceased including:

- Full name
- Date of birth
- Passport number
- Where and when the passport was issued
- Details of the next of kin if you are not the closest relative

Bringing the body home

If you wish to bring the body back to the UK, British Consular staff will help by putting you in touch with the international funeral director. The body will need to be embalmed and placed in a zinc-lined coffin before it can be removed from the country. It may take some time to bring the body home, especially if a post-mortem examination is held. Before you can bring the body home you will need a certified English translation of the foreign death certificate form the country in which the person died, authorization to remove the deceased's body from the country and a certificate of embalming. The British Consul can help to arrange this documentation.

Funeral costs

If the deceased's funeral costs are covered by travel insurance, contact the insurance company straight away. They will then contact the funeral directors for you and make the necessary arrangements. If the costs are not covered then all the costs concerned, including repatriation of the body and possessions will be borne by the deceased's estate.

Arranging the funeral in the UK

You will need to take an authenticated translation of the death certificate to the register office in the area you intend to hold the funeral. The registrar will then issue a 'certificate of no liability to register'. This certificate is usually given to the funeral director to enable the funeral to go ahead. The certificate is not required if a coroner has issued a Certificate E for Cremation or an Order for Burial.

If you wish to have the body cremated, you will need a Cremation Order (or a form E if there was a post-mortem) before you start planning the funeral.

Having a funeral abroad

You can arrange for the burial or cremation in the country where the person died. The British Consulate can give you information about this.

Deaths in disasters abroad

If the deceased has been killed in a disaster abroad, natural or otherwise, ask the Foreign and Commonwealth Office for help. They will provide support and advice. The main enquiry number is 020 7008 1500. The deceased will need to be identified and you may be asked for information about them including a physical description, name and address of the person's UK doctor or dentist.

The police may also need a photograph and/or fingerprint samples from the deceased's house.

Going to see someone who has died

If you choose to have the person who has died looked after at the undertakers, you may well want to visit them. Spending time with someone who has died isn't everyone's choice. Visiting someone who has died gives you:

- Time to accept what has happened.
- Time to let go.
- Time to take in the fact that your world has changed.
- Time to say what you have to say.

■ Time to see that person looking peaceful, not as they were when they had just died.

If you think that it is a difficult thing to do, consider that people who do go to see someone after death are often the better for it. If the body has been badly injured you can still go and visit. Your funeral director may be able to make the body presentable. If not arrange for the body to be covered except, say, for a hand. Or you can arrange for the coffin to be covered.

****

Ch. 2

Steps after Registration

If you need to make arrangements in relation to the dead person's estate, then you will need to obtain several copies of the certified death certificate. You will find that a separate certificate is needed for application for probate, for dealing with banks and insurance company's etc. Before applying for the death certificate then you should estimate how many you are likely to need.

It is important that you notify the Department of Work and Pensions and any other relevant agency about the death (through the Tell us Once service outlined in depth in chapter 10), as you will need to decide about pensions etc. There may be several other benefits that you can claim after death, including help with funeral costs from the social fund. The funeral director may have a stock of the appropriate forms, which you must fill in.

In addition to copies of the death certificate, the registrar will provide another certificate, known as the green certificate, to say that the death is now registered, and a funeral can go ahead. The funeral director cannot proceed without it. If the coroner is or has been involved in the death then a different process takes place, which will be outlined a little later. If a registrar's certificate has been issued before registration, then the deceased can be buried only. If it has been issued after registration, then it can be cremated. The funeral director will forward the certificate either to the cemetery authority or to the vicar of the appropriate churchyard or to the office of the local crematorium.

Copies of a death certificate can be obtained later from the superintendent registrar if more than one month has elapsed, or from the registrar if still relatively soon after the date of death. Applications for certificates by post can be made to the general register office, see addresses at the rear of this book.

In Northern Ireland it should be made to the Registrar General. There is a fee, again relatively minor and a stamped addressed envelope will be needed.

Scotland: Ordering a Certificate

Currently, at the time of writing, the onsite registration services are closed during the pandemic. The below is an extract from the ScotlandsPeople website: www.scotlandspeople.gov.uk

"Customers can order a certificate using Certificates and Copies on our ScotlandsPeople website:

https://www.scotlandspeople.gov.uk. Certificate ordering will be available online Monday to Friday between 9 am and 4.30 pm.

We have removed our priority ordering channel and we will do our best to complete orders as soon as we can however this may not be within our usual timescales.

We can only process online orders and will not be able to process those received by any other contact channel.

We understand that there may be very urgent cases where certificates are required quickly. If this is the case, please order the certificate online and then use our contact form on ScotlandsPeople selecting 'Certificates and Copies' to provide information on your urgent requirements and one of our team will respond directly.

For urgent Adoption Birth Certificates and No Trace Divorce Letters, these can be requested through the Contact Us button, on the ScotlandsPeople website.

****

Ch. 3

Taking Decisions about a Funeral-Practical and Financial Considerations

---

Understandably, those closest to the deceased wish to get the funeral over with as soon as is practically possible. This is a reaction to the death and to bury a person is to disassociate from the trauma of death, or at least from the first manifestations. However, it is important in all cases to ensure that a decent burial is arranged.

In some cases, the bereaved person will have left instructions in a will concerning burial. There is no strict legal obligation to go by the wishes of the deceased, however, although it is usual to do so. If no instructions were left, then the burial arrangements will usually be arranged by the next of kin or an executor of a will. If no next of kin can be traced and there is no executor, the hospital will accept responsibility to arrange a minimum priced funeral. Although any capable person can organise a funeral, it is usual in times such as this to enlist the help of a funeral director.

A funeral director by another name is an undertaker. As with all professions, there are associations regulating the activities of funeral directors, namely The National Association of Funeral Directors, The Funeral Standards Council and the National Society of Allied and Independent Funeral Directors. You should make sure that a funeral director chosen by you belongs to one of the above associations. If you choose an unregistered firm, there may be no comeback in cases of future problems. The function of the funeral director is to assume complete responsibility for organising and supplying all that is needed for a funeral and to provide as much care as is possible for relatives at this difficult time. Some funeral directors will also offer a bereavement counselling service. It is up to the deceased's family to organise a funeral and contact a director, not the executor of an estate, although in practice the executor will take on this function if requested.

A funeral director will provide a quote for a funeral, and you should be clear about this at the outset. As with all services there are varying degrees of service at different prices. Insurance can be taken out for a funeral during an individual's lifetime and there are several so-called friendly societies who offer plans.

Any scheme that you invest in, as with all savings schemes has to be regulated and in the case of funeral plans the regulatory body is the National Association of Pre-Paid Funeral Plans, address and general contact details at the back of this book.

From July 29th, 2022, it will be a requirement to register with the Financial Conduct Authority (see more on page 58).

If there is a problem with money, this should be discussed with the funeral director who can assist by encouraging you to apply for a grant from the benefits agency. Normally however, the cost of a funeral is paid for from the deceased's estate.

How to find a funeral director

You shouldn't just pick the first one you find. Call around and get at least two quotes before you choose one that's best for you.

You should also consider using a local independent funeral director. They're usually cheaper than a national chain. Use these sites to find a local funeral director. Make sure you check more than one Funeral site (there are many) as the prices will vary.

Fair Funerals Campaign

Go to https://fairfuneralscampaign.org who will help you to locate a funeral director near you. You could also use the Funeral Choice website https://www.yourfuneralchoice.com to compare the price of your local funeral directors. You can refine the results by changing your search area. The prices shown don't include the cremation or burial fee.

Costs of a funeral

There has been much in the news recently (2022) about the costs of funerals and how there is a move by some companies, such as Co-operative Funeral Care to enter the market with lower overall costs. One of the biggest providers of funerals, Dignity, has been forced to reconsider its prices after the Co-op cut the average cost of a funeral to £1895 in England and £1675 in Scotland. The prices include collection and preparation of the body and the services of a Hearse. However, there are other costs to consider which increases the overall cost.

Funeral Plans and other plans such as insurance
Why use a funeral plan?

Many people worry that when they die, they won't leave enough money for their funeral and their loved ones will be left with the bill. With a funeral plan, you arrange and pay for it in advance, so your relatives don't have to cover all the cost themselves. You can arrange a funeral plan for your own funeral or for someone else's if it's held in the UK.

With a standard funeral plan, you pay for your funeral in advance, at today's prices. You can pay the plan provider in either a lump sum or instalments. You can buy a plan from most funeral directors.

Funeral plans vary in terms of what's included. All plans include the services of a funeral director who takes care of the deceased, arranges the funeral, and organises transport. However, there are differences with the additional services that plans offer. Some may provide high-quality coffins, access to view the deceased in a chapel of rest, and limousines to transport guests to the funeral. Other plans may be more basic.

As well as the core costs of the funeral director and coffin, funeral plans will also include – or make a provision for – third-party costs. These can include the cost of using a crematorium, doctors' fees and the cost of a minister or celebrant. These third-party costs are usually called 'disbursements'.

If you're buying a cremation funeral plan, it won't usually cover the cost of disbursements in full. Instead, they're covered by an allowance, which rises in line with inflation. However, there's a risk that if funeral costs rise faster than inflation, there won't be quite enough money in your plan to cover these costs. This would leave your family or estate with extra to pay when you die. Some funeral plans offer a guarantee to cover all third-party costs.

If you're opting for a burial funeral plan, it will usually include the cost of digging the grave. But the cost of the burial plot – as well as extras such as headstones – won't be included.

Funeral plans never include the cost of flowers or organising a wake. But some plans allow you to put aside some extra money to cover these costs.

It's important to make sure you know what your plan does and doesn't provide before you pay.

How safe is money in a funeral plan?

Your money must either be invested in a trust fund with trustees, or in an insurance policy, which is then used to pay for the funeral. Funeral plans aren't currently regulated, but the government has announced plans to bring them under regulation by the Financial Conduct Authority. From July 29th, 2022, all funeral plan providers must be regulated by the Financial Conduct Authority. One large provider, Safe Hands, has recently had its application to be registered turned down. In this case, it should stop selling funeral plans. This will be the case for several Funeral Plan providers and if you have a plan, you should contact your provider to discuss the matter.

When regulation begins, Consumers will be able to complain to the Financial Services Ombudsman if there is a problem and the plans that have been bought will be protected by the Financial Services Compensation Scheme.

For now, until the 29th of July 2022, the industry relies on a voluntary regulator called the Funeral Planning Authority

(FPA). They don't offer the same level of protection for customers as a government regulator, but they do have a set of standards their members have to follow. They also help to resolve customer complaints. Make sure that you only buy plans from companies that are part of the FPA. You can check their list of members on the FPA website.

If you're paying for your funeral plan in a lump sum, you could consider paying for part of it on your credit card. When you pay with your credit card, you can get extra protection if things go wrong with the funeral director. You could also get this protection if you were to pay at least £100 on your credit card, and then pay the rest in instalments. If you die before you've finished paying the instalments, your family or estate will need to pay the balance. Some plans offer to pay the remaining instalments through a form of insurance.

Pros and cons of funeral plans
Pros:

- Funeral plans give you the chance to make the arrangements that you want for your funeral. They protect you against rising costs.

Cons:

- They can be expensive. Even if you're paying in instalments, they're likely to cost at least £20 a month –

and often considerably more. If funeral prices fall, you could end up overpaying for your funeral. Some plans don't guarantee all the costs. Funeral plans aren't currently regulated.

Questions to ask the plan provider

- Are there any cancellation charges?
- What exactly is included in the plan and what potential costs are not?
- Could there be any other expenses for the funeral, and what happens if there are?
- Is it possible to cancel the plan if circumstances change, for example if you've arranged for your spouse's funeral but you later separate?
- Does the plan allow you to choose the funeral director?
- What if your chosen funeral director goes out of business?
- What happens if the person the funeral is intended for dies abroad or away from home?
- Can the funeral director arrange a funeral of a different standard from the one you've chosen?
- If you pay by instalments, how long do you do this for and do you have to pay interest?

- What happens if there are outstanding instalments at death?
- What freedom do you have to change the details of your funeral plan?
- How does the funeral planning company know about the plan holder's death?

Over 50s plans

Over 50s plans are insurance policies that guarantee to pay out when you die. You pay a fixed amount every month for the rest of your life. In most cases, the payout doesn't rise with inflation. They can be poor value if you live a long life – as you'll end up paying in much more than you'll get out. However, they may be right for you if you can't afford a funeral plan and you don't trust yourself to save for your funeral in a savings account, without spending the money on something else.

Pros and cons of over 50s plans

Pros: Over 50s plans don't need any medical underwriting. This means that being in poor health makes no difference to your pay out. You can pay as much as you can afford – unlike funeral plans where minimum premiums are much higher.

Cons: In most cases, you lose your whole payout, and you won't get any money back, if you stop paying in the first few

61

years. However, some providers are now offering payment holidays–to give you some breathing space if you're struggling to keep up with payments. And a growing number of policies will still protect some of your payout if you stop paying after a certain number of years.

- The payout on most plans doesn't increase with inflation. This means many people end up paying more in premiums than their payout.
- Whole of Life insurance could pay out more than 40% more when you die than an over 50s plan – according to Which?.
- You usually need to survive beyond the first two years of an over 50s plan to get the full payout.
- Some plans require you to continue paying premiums until you die. This means that if you live a very long time, you could pay far more in premiums than you'll get back.

If you do decide to take out a funeral plan or over 50s plan, keep the paperwork in a safe place and make sure your next of kin know about it. Also, check that they are regulated by the Financial Conduct Authority.

Alternatives to funeral plans and over 50s plans

Putting money into a savings account

Putting a little money aside each month is one straightforward way to save for a funeral. This isn't risk-free though, as you may die before you build up enough to pay for a funeral. And many people worry that they may not have the discipline to leave their savings untouched.

Using the money you leave behind in your will

You may have assets that can be sold when you die, such as your house. You could make it clear in your will that you want these to be used to pay for your funeral. However, it can take some time for properties to be sold after someone dies. See chapter 10 for more information concerning disposal of property.

So it's worth talking to the family member who you want to arrange your funeral and checking that they have enough to pay upfront.

Death in service from an employer

Some employers provide a payout if you die whilst you're still working for them. If you're a member of a trade union, professional body or other association, they might pay a benefit when a member dies. Contact them to find out.

Life insurance

Using the lump sum payment from a life insurance policy can pay for a funeral. According to the Association of British Insurers, payments are generally made about a month after the policyholder dies. It could be longer if the death needs to be investigated.

More information about funerals

The sources of information differ depending on where you live:

For England and Wales, visit GOV.UK

For Northern Ireland, visit nidirect

For Scotland, visit www.mygov.scot/

In addition, Ageuk offer useful advice on planning for funerals www.ageuk.org.uk

The price of a funeral will consist of two elements, the fees that the director pays out on the client's behalf-doctors' fees, cremation fees if appropriate, fees for the minister, burial fees, gravediggers, flowers and so on. These are the people who provide a service and must be paid. Then there is the fee charged by the funeral director, removal of the deceased, preparation and arrangements, use of the chapel of rest, the hearse and limousine and bearers and so on. Notwithstanding the ongoing price war, the overall average cost of a funeral with a traditional burial is £4,257 and the average cost of a funeral with cremation is £3,311. This will, of course, vary depending on specific choices and circumstances.

When breaking this down, there is a usual minimum price for a funeral starting with a basic funeral for around £700 plus any disbursements, usually around £300-600 for a cremation and more for a burial due to the increase in activities necessary. As far as price goes, cremation is most certainly cheaper. The average cost is around £300 as opposed for around £400 for a burial. Fees for burials will vary according to the whereabouts of the cemetery. A Church of England Burial tends to be marginally cheaper than others but most graveyards have little burial space left, often involving a second internment in a grave. Some funeral directors will charge for a complete service, including coffin while others will make a separate charge for the choice of coffin required. Funeral director will be able to show clients a range of types of coffins. The material that a coffin is made from varies and will greatly affect the price. Basic coffins are made from chipboard laminated with plastic foil. More expensive coffins are made from solid wood, usually oak. There are other coffins, made from strong cardboard. However, it is always best to closely inspect the type of coffin you intend to purchase and ask questions about its durability.

Whether you buy a coffin for a cremation or for a burial will also have some bearing on the type that you buy as weaker coffins will normally suffice for cremation. Each coffin must be fitted with a nameplate of the deceased. The plate will also usually contain the age and date of death.

Associated costs

The overall cost of a funeral will consist of the funeral directors' own fees and those paid to other as disbursements. However, there may well be extra costs, which are not paid direct to the funeral director, or if paid cover anything extra such as long journeys in limousines, special services etc. Any funeral director should supply you with a breakdown of what a funeral will cost before the funeral. Funeral directors will always explain different charges and conditions in various areas so that you have an idea of costs. It may well be that you decide that you wish to eliminate certain parts of the service to keep costs down. There are fees for Church of England Services service and for a burial in the churchyard. It is always necessary to ascertain the exact cost from the funeral director. Fees for burial in a municipal city cemetery are likely to be a lot more than this.

Overall Burial Fees as at 2022-for more information visit Church of England Parochial Fees 2022 | Law & Religion UK (lawandreligionuk.com)

Monuments

These normally range from £49 to £150 depending on the type and size of the monument required. The general definition of a 'monument' as including headstone, cross, kerb, border, vase, chain, railing, tablet, plaque, marker, flatstone, tombstone or monument or tomb of any other kind.

Obtaining help with funeral costs

If a person is on low income and is in difficulties over funeral expenses there is help from the social fund administered by the Department of Work and Pensions, although such help is subject to rigid criteria. The applicant or applicants partner must be in receipt of one or more benefits, Income support, Income based Job seekers allowance, Pension Credit, Housing Benefit, Working Tax Credit where a Disability or Severe Disability element is included or Child Tax Credit which is at a higher rate than the family element.. This applies only to the person arranging the funeral. And the person applying for the benefit must be the one arranging the funeral, the next of kin or person described as the next of kin. The benefit is means tested, and if there are savings (check amounts) these will be considered when assessing the grant. If there is a close relative able to pay the costs of the funeral, then an award will not usually be made. More details of the benefits available can be obtained from:

www.gov.uk/government/organisations/department-for-work-pensions

This is the Department of Work and Pensions website. If money becomes available out of the deceased's estate, then this will be used to pay back the funeral expenses provided by the social fund. The benefits agency form is the SF200, and the funeral director can also help with this.

The Social Fund Payment will make provision for up to £1000 towards the funeral directors' fees, which must encompass almost all the costs. In addition, a cremation fee will be paid and the costs of certain doctor's forms. Although other small payments are made for necessary expenses the money only provides for a simple dignified funeral. Other extras, which may be desired, are not covered. See chapter 8 for more details of benefits available. The rules for Scotland and Northern Ireland will differ. Some local authorities provide a municipal funeral service. The cost is very much less than the average local funeral and details can be obtained from your local authority. Those relatives of a member of the armed forces who die in service may be able to receive help with funeral costs from the Ministry of Defence.

Where a person dies without relatives, or no one can be traced then the local authority where the person died, or hospital if appropriate, will arrange a simple funeral. Many hospitals maintain a funeral fund and local authorities usually have close links with funeral directors.

****

Ch. 4

The Burial-Main Points

Anyone, whether Christian or not, whose address is within the ecclesiastical parish is, in theory at least, entitled to be buried within the parish churchyard, even if a death occurs away from the parish. Some churches have burial grounds away from the church, where parishioners have the right of burial. Ex-parishioners and non-parishioners with family graves in a parish area have a right to be buried within a particular parish. It is the local vicar or parish priest who will make the decision about burial and how much to charge. In London, certain special rules exist, under the London local Authorities Act 2007, concerning burials.

Those who are resident within the local parish must pay a fee to the local church for a funeral service in church and burial in a churchyard. There are fees payable for a funeral service in a church and these should be checked with the local church. These fees change on an annual basis and are decided by the church. If the church service is followed by burial in a municipal or private cemetery, then the fee remains the same. There is a fee for a burial in a churchyard without having had a service beforehand. No fee is payable for the burial of a stillborn child or for the funeral or burial of an infant who died within one year of birth. If the ashes are to be buried in a churchyard following cremation, there is a fee and if there is to be a further service following cremation then a fee will be payable. This fee does not apply if there is a simple service of committal. There are additional fees, such as grave diggers fees, this being up to £100. This can be more expensive if a funeral director provides the gravedigger.

A vicar will allot the site of a grave in a churchyard. The burial fee does not entitle anyone to the ownership of the grave or any rights of burial there. If you want the exclusive use of a particular plot in a graveyard, you must apply to the diocesan register to reserve a grave space. This is by the grant of a licence called a faculty. The freehold of the ground, in all circumstances belongs to the church. Normally it takes about six weeks for a faculty to be granted. A faculty must be applied for before death. It is too late after death.

Burial in cemeteries

Most cemeteries are non-denominational and are run and managed by either a local authority or a privately owned company. Particular Denominations own a few cemeteries in the U.K and burial places are restricted to members of that denomination. Some cemeteries will have a section of the ground consecrated by the Church of England, while the opening of new cemeteries is attended by a service of consecration for the whole area. The fee payable to a member of the Church of England Clergy for holding a ceremony is the same as that for a funeral service in a church. There will be no church fee.

Some cemeteries have ground dedicated to, or reserved for other specific religious groups, and a separate section of general ground. In most cemeteries any type of religious service, or non-service at all, can be held. Many cemeteries have a chapel in which non-denominational services can be held. Some cemeteries will provide the services of a chaplain for burial services on a rota basis. There is usually a choice of Church of England, Free Church or Roman Catholic.

Fees for burial in a cemetery vary according to where it is and who owns it. Fees are usually displayed at the cemetery. It is necessary to make enquiries as to what the fees cover and to obtain an itemised estimate of cost. In most local authority cemeteries, a higher fee is required for those who are not resident within the area. These can be double or treble the normal fees.

Cemetery fees are divided into two parts: there is a charge for purchasing the exclusive rights of burial in a particular plot and an additional charge for internment. These charges will vary considerably. Most local authority cemeteries have an application form which the executor or next of kin is required to fill in. All fees must be paid before the funeral and all documents sent. Normally, as stated this will usually be dealt with by a funeral director.

Types of graves

There are different categories of grave in a cemetery. At the one end of the scale are graves without exclusive rights of burial. The person paying for a burial has no rights to say who else may be buried in the grave. The graves are given a number, marked by a number and usually it is not allowed to put up a plaque by the grave. In a few cemeteries, for a small fee a grave space can be reserved for a specific period from the date of payment. After this time, it reverts to the cemetery. In most cemeteries it is possible to buy the right to a specific plot for a period usually not exceeding 50 years. Obviously, this is more expensive than the other options.

For a private grave, a deed of grant is given for which cemeteries make a small charge. Another type of grave is what is known as the "lawn grave" in which a person has the right to exclusive burial but can put up a simple headstone leaving the rest of the grave as grass.

This grave is easier to maintain, and a lot of modern cemeteries allow lawn graves only.

Other burial places

If you want to be buried in ground other than churchyard ground, then the law stipulates that such burials be registered. The deeds to land, even freehold, may impose restrictions on use and enquiries should be made to local authority Environmental Health and Planning Departments. There is the right in certain circumstances to a burial at sea which will be discussed a little later. In addition, there is what is known as "woodland burial" where plots are made available in meadowland or other woodland No burial plaque or stone is normally permitted and the emphasis is on the maintenance of a natural environment.

Cremation

Most funerals involve the act of cremation rather than burial. As discussed earlier, cremation cannot take place until the correct certificates have been produced and the death registered. Four statutory forms must be completed before cremation can take place: one by the next of kin or the executor, the others by three different doctors. Forms are issued by the crematorium. Both funeral directors and doctors normally keep a supply. The first form, form A is an application for cremation and must be completed by the next of kin or the executor and countersigned by a householder who knows that person personally. Forms B and C are on the

75

same piece of paper and must be completed by the doctor who attended the deceased during the last illness.

Form C is the confirmatory medical certificate and must be completed by a doctor who has been a medical practitioner (registered) for five years or more in the United Kingdom. Doctors must not be related to the deceased or work on the same ward if they are hospital workers. In other words, they should be independent of each other.

Form F is the fourth statutory document which must be signed by the medical referee of the crematorium, stating that he or she is satisfied with the details on forms B and C, or the coroner's certificate for cremation. The medical referee can prevent cremation taking place and can order a post-mortem to take place or refer the matter to the coroner. Relatives have no right to prevent this post-mortem. If they do not want it to take place, then they must bury the deceased instead.

When the coroner is involved and has ordered a post-mortem, he or she will issue a certificate for cremation. Forms B and C are not required. When a death is reported to the coroner, he or she must be informed at the outset if the funeral is to involve cremation, so that the appropriate certificate can be issued. This is form E and will be supplied as a pink form to the relatives so that they may register and as a yellow form to the funeral director for submission to the crematorium.

If the body of a stillborn child is to be cremated, a special medical certificate must be issued by a doctor who was present at the birth, or who examined the body after birth. No second medical certificate is required, but the medical referee still must complete form F. Many crematoria do not charge for the cremation of stillborn children, or infants up to the age of one year.

Fees for cremation

Fees include the charges made by the crematorium, the fees for the doctor's certificates and usually a standard fee for the minister who takes the service. An organist also needs to be paid in addition to other costs. The funeral director will usually pay all fees and charge accordingly. Crematorium fees on average are from £600 with extra fees for those who did not reside in the district of cremation. Doctors who prepare initial forms will usually charge a minimum fee which rises each year.

On occasions, when death has occurred in a hospital, the hospital will wish to carry out a post- mortem to improve their knowledge of the patient's condition. The consent of relatives must be given and if so, form C will not be required-providing the post-mortem was carried out by a pathologist of not less than five years standing and the result known by the doctor who completed form B. Only one fee will be charged, unless the pathologist was less than five years standing, in which case another doctor must complete form C and the full fee will be charged. Most crematoria charge reduced fees for children up to school leaving age. You should check the above fees as they change subject to notice.

Most crematoria are run by local authorities, although private crematoria do exist. Each has its scale of fees and offers a brochure of services and fees, usually having an open day for the public, usually Sunday, as crematoria are open only from Monday to Friday, with occasional Saturdays.

Services in a crematorium

Charges for a crematorium will normally include the chapel, whether or not it is used. Chapels are non-denominational, catering for a variety of religions. Music can be chosen by the relatives. If they wish, relatives can opt for a non-religious funeral. Funeral directors can usually refer you to someone who can organise this.

Cremations and memorials

Most crematoriums will have various forms of memorial. There will be a book of remembrance in which the name of the deceased can be inscribed. Other memorials involve wall plaques, memorial flowers or rose bushes. There will usually be an extra charge for this. Some more sophisticated crematoria have extensive means of remembrance in their landscaped gardens. Again, there will be a charge for this.

Remains

Cremated remains or ashes of the deceased may be scattered in the grounds of the crematorium, taken away to be scattered elsewhere or buried in a local churchyard or cemetery. The crematorium will not usually charge a fee for scattering ashes after a funeral. However, a fee will be charged if ashes are stored and scattered later. There will usually be a fee if the ashes are to be scattered in a crematorium to the one where the funeral took place. There is a Church of England Charge for the burial of ashes in a churchyard. This is around £150, at current prices, increasing annually. However, these prices should be checked with the relevant church.

A useful leaflet concerning cremation, "Questions People ask" is available from some local crematoria.

Direct Cremation

Direct cremation is offered by some companies - where the body is collected from a mortuary during normal working hours and cremated at a convenient time. There's usually no viewing or ceremony beforehand, or a limousine for the family and mourners. And if you wish to have the ashes afterwards, make sure you request them. You usually need to collect them, but some might deliver for a charge. This then leaves you to hold a ceremony, if you wish, at a time and place of your choosing.

Costs of a direct cremation

A budget of about £1,600 is suggested. There are several companies online offering direct cremation for around £1,000. This price normally includes third party costs such as doctor's certification and crematorium fees. If you'd like to have the ashes returned to you, this can cost an extra £100. And collecting the body outside of normal working hours, or from a nursing home or residence, is about an extra £500. This brings the total cost of a direct cremation to £1,600. Costs might vary depending on location.

So, shop around and check whether the company offers a reasonable price for covering your area.

If you choose to hold a ceremony afterwards, you'll need to factor in these costs as well. However, there are a variety of low-cost ways to have a ceremony, such as having it at home.

How to find one a provider of direct cremations

You can do an online search for 'direct cremation' in your area. If you're in England or Wales, you could try these national providers:

- Woodland Wishes
- Simplicity Cremations
- Simplicita Cremations
- Pure Cremation
- Memoria

Or use these sites below to find a local provider.

- Fair Funerals Campaign
- The National Association of Funeral Directors
- The Society of Allied and Independent Funeral Directors

Make sure you check more than one site as they will show different results. Some might not provide direct cremations.

****

Ch.5

The Events Before a Funeral

Most funeral directors maintain a 24-hour service. If death occurs at home or in a nursing home, two funeral directors will arrive rapidly and take the body to the mortuary. It is rare for a body to remain at home between death and the funeral although is possible if requested by relatives. It is recommended that a funeral director be approached as soon as is possible after a death.

When a body is taken by a funeral director then it will lie in a chapel of rest, where the body will lie in a coffin before the funeral. Laying out of a body will almost always take place in the funeral director mortuary. Arrangements need to be made about any jewellery and clothes, as the funeral director can supply a gown if necessary. If a person dies in hospital the body is usually taken to the hospital mortuary-although a few hospitals normally subcontract mortuary facilities to a funeral director. When a body is removed by a funeral director it will lie until cremation papers have been completed. If a coroner has decided that a post-mortem is necessary, then the body will be taken to the mortuary in preparation.

When a body is kept in a chapel of rest, relatives and friends can go to see it before the funeral. Sometimes, there will be an extra charge to see the body at evenings and weekends. Some larger firms of funeral directors also have chapels for private prayer, in which a religious service can be held at the beginning of the funeral before the cortege leaves for the cemetery or crematorium.

Embalming a body

The process of embalming is intended to delay the process of decomposition of a body. The blood in a body is replaced with a preservative, normally a solution of formalin. This is like a blood transfusion. It is necessary to embalm a body if it is returned to a private house to await a funeral or if the funeral is to be held more than five days after a death and cannot be put into cold storage. Before a body can be embalmed, a doctor must have completed the medical certificate of the cause of death and the death registered.

When cremation is involved, forms B and C must also have been completed. If the coroner is involved, then embalming cannot take place unless permission has been obtained. Embalmers are qualified and no one else other than a qualified person should be used.

The final arrangements before a funeral

The funeral director must have the registrar's disposal certificate before confirming the final arrangements. All the functions connected with burial or cremation must have been completed and all fees paid.

The funeral director or a member of the family should ask whomever the family wishes to officiate at the service whether they can or are willing to do so, and at the allotted time or date. Services can be held in a church, churchyard, cemetery, crematorium chapel, village hall or any other suitable place. Funeral services can be held anywhere, with no form of licensing necessary.

Non-Church of England Funerals

Denominational burial grounds usually insist on their own form of service. For a practicing Roman Catholic it is usual for a priest to say a requiem mass in the local parish church and for the priest to take the funeral service.

With Orthodox Jews, the body should be buried as soon as possible once the disposal certificate has been issued. If a man subscribes to a synagogue burial society, he or his wife and children will be buried free by the society in its cemetery. Orthodox Jews are never cremated, and embalming or bequeathing a body for medical purposes is never allowed. There are usually no flowers. The burial is simple. Reform non-orthodox Jews are not so rigid and permit cremation and flowers. If a Jew dies away from home, it is the responsibility of the relatives to bring the body back at their own expense for the synagogue burial society to take over.

Non-religious services

There is no obligation to have a ceremony at a funeral. It is important to communicate this to the executor or person in charge if this is the case. If a body is to be buried in a churchyard without a religious ceremony, or by someone of another denomination, you should give at least 48 hours notice in writing. Usual fees are still applicable. If the body is to be buried in a cemetery or cremated without religious ceremony, the funeral director or local authority should be informed. If there is to be no ceremony, then usually a few members will attend the funeral and there will be a few minutes silence or with some music played.

Announcements of deaths are usually made in local papers. Sometimes, the national dailies will have an announcement. The address of the deceased should never be inserted in the obituary. A lot of houses have been broken into when a funeral takes place. The press notice should stipulate requirements for the giving of money to the deceased's favourite charity and for flowers. The time and date and other arrangements for the funeral are included, and these details should be tailored to a family's requirements. When a body is buried, flowers are normally left on a grave after it has been filled in. At a crematorium there will normally be restrictions as to where flowers can be placed.

The funeral

Although it was tradition for the cortege (procession) to travel from the house to the place of the funeral it is just as common, given the prominence of the funeral director, for the funeral to begin from the premises of the funeral director. If the funeral director provides cars for the relatives and friends of the deceased, then he or she will organise and marshal the event and arrange departure.

The funeral director should have discussed all the details of the funeral with the family beforehand, and also arrange where people are to be taken after the funeral and also take care of other last-minute arrangements. The funeral director may walk in front of the hearse as it leaves the deceased's house, and as it approaches the church or crematorium. This is both a mark of respect to the deceased and a practical arrangement so he can direct the traffic. The coffin will be usually carried into the church or crematorium on the shoulders (or by handles on the coffin) of the funeral director's staff.

Sometimes members of the family act as bearers. Occasionally, at the more formal funeral, pallbearers walk alongside the coffin.

The burial

If a burial is preceded by a service in church, the coffin is taken into the church by the bearers and placed in front of the altar. In Roman Catholic churches the coffin is taken into the church before the funeral and remains there until the funeral takes place. After the service the bearers will take the coffin from the church to the churchyard or cemetery. If a burial is not preceded by a church service, then the coffin is taken directly from the hearse to the cemetery. The coffin is lowered into the grave while the words of committal are said. A register of burial in the parish area is kept by the church. Copies can be obtained for a small fee.

When someone is buried in a Church of England churchyard, the family is responsible for the grave. Municipal and private cemeteries will employ grounds men to look after the common parts and graves. Cemeteries often stipulate the provision of a simple grave to keep costs of maintenance down. A lot of churches have restrictions on the type of headstones and memorials used and it will be necessary to check with the church first before making any decisions.

Cremation

Traditionally, the funeral service prior to cremation was held in church, with the congregation travelling to the crematorium for a brief committal afterwards. It is an increasing practice for funeral services to be held entirely in a crematorium chapel. When the words of committal are spoken, the coffin passes out of site although some mourners prefer the coffin to remain until the last mourner has left the chapel.

During the funeral service, the funeral directors' staff will take flowers from the hearse and place them in the floral display area. The funeral director will take appropriate flowers to a hospital or nursing homes after the mourners have left. When the coffin is out of site it is taken to the committal room to await cremation. When the cremation process is complete the ashes are refined separately and placed in containers.

In the process of deciding arrangements for the cremation, the next of kin or executors of the deceased person's estate can ask to be present when the coffin is placed in the cremator. This is especially relevant for Hindu funerals where traditionally the next of kin would light the funeral pyre. Usually, only two people are allowed. Each crematorium will keep a register of cremations and again a copy can be obtained for a small fee. When deciding arrangements for a funeral, clients are asked what they would like to do with the ashes.

While most ashes are scattered or buried in the crematorium grounds, they can also be removed by next of kin to be scattered or buried elsewhere. When ashes are removed, the crematorium will normally provide a certificate confirming that the cremation has taken place. If ashes are to be scattered in the grounds of a different crematorium, there will be a fee of up to £30. There is no law regulating the disposal of ashes, they can be scattered anywhere, with consent from owners etc.

Burial in Scotland

In Scotland it is possible to purchase the exclusive rights to burial in a cemetery or churchyard (Kirkyard) plot. A grave is called a lair. Kirkyards are administered by the local district or islands council. Regulations and procedures for cremation are the same as in England and Wales.

Arranging a funeral without a funeral director

It is possible to arrange a funeral without using a funeral director. Most people will want a funeral director to take care of matters after death, due to grief and the wish to arrange matters quickly. However, some people prefer to arrange their own funeral.

If the coroner is not involved, a doctor's certificate as to the cause of death must be obtained and the death registered.

The appropriate papers must be obtained and sent to the cemetery or crematorium with a fee. A date and time for the funeral must be arranged. A minister should be approached if they are to conduct the funeral. A coffin must be obtained along with the means of conveying the coffin to the funeral. If a burial is taking place a gravedigger must be hired

With cremation, the papers, as outlined in this book, must be obtained and a coffin and crematoria arrangements made. Coffins can be purchased from funeral supermarkets or from a funeral director. It is always highly advisable to purchase a coffin and not attempt to make one yourself. Biodegradable coffins can also be purchased for a low price. These are normally made of cardboard. Details can be obtained from the natural death centre, address at the back of this book.

It is possible to arrange for a burial to take place on your own land-in a garden or a field. Planning permission is not necessary. However, there are other restrictions, one being the level of the water table and if this is likely to be affected. Other difficulties can arise, one being if a family or person decides to move house. A Home Office Licence is required to exhume a body.

As stated, although it is possible to carry out a funeral yourself, without a funeral director, it is not a common occurrence because of the amount of work involved. Many people decide to leave this to a funeral director. At this point, it is worth outlining the practice of 'Green Funerals' as this is the choice of people who are either into environmentally friendly funerals or natural burials, where communing with nature is paramount.

Green funerals

A green funeral is an ethical choice and one that seeks not to harm the environment. It is also, for some, an aesthetic choice, which may appeal to those who have no environmental interests but rejects the traditional stuffy funeral in favour of an outdoors, homespun, back to nature feel. It prefers an unspoilt landscape to that of a regimented ceremony.

A Real Green funeral

The elements of a real green funeral are as follows:

- Rejection of cremation
- Opts for burial in a site serving a conservation purpose
- Creates a site which is not visually definable as a burial ground
- Reviles embalming
- Requires a coffin or shroud locally made from natural sustainable material
- Buries the body at a depth where it can decompose aerobically
- Rejects bought flowers, prefers garden flowers (if any)

- ■ Forbids demarcation of the grave
- ■ Forbids marking or personalizing of the grave with any sort of permanent memorial
- ■ Forbids tending of the grave
- ■ Discourages visits to the grave unless on foot or bike.

A real green funeral leaves no trace behind. However, there are at present very few burial sites that meet the above criteria. Most people who favour a natural burial want their decomposed body to nourish the plants and soil around it. Natural burial is a very personal form of recycling. Many like the idea of a tree planted on top of them. In a local authority cemetery, by law, no part of a coffin must be less than three feet below the surface except where soil conditions allow, in which case two feet will do. This is too deep to ensure truly vibrant aerobic decomposition. This law does not apply to private burial grounds. However, the Ministry of Justice is urging compliance. Almost all natural burial grounds bury bodies at a depth where decomposition will be cold, slow, and mostly anaerobic.

There are pluses and minuses when considering a green/natural burial as opposed to a conventional funeral. The Association of Natural Burial Grounds lists all green grounds in the UK. This site can also point the way to organizations that can give you more advice. Details can be found at the Natural Death Centre below.

The Natural Death Centre

The Natural Death Centre is a charity which campaigns for a change in social attitudes to death and dying. The philosophy of the NDC grew out of that of the natural childbirth movement. The NDC believes that tasking control; and keeping interventions by strangers to a minimum improves the quality of dying for the dying person and its impact on his or her carers. In the matter of caring for the dead it believes that taking control is therapeutic.

The NDC encourages and supports those who want to arrange environmentally friendly and inexpensive funerals, and it is behind the Association of Natural Burial Grounds – anbg.co.uk.

A hands-on approach to dealing with the dying and the dead strongly appeals to people of all sorts who know their own minds and like to do things their own way.

The NDC publishes The Natural Death Handbook, which is full of practical advice and personal stories. It operates a telephone helpline and offers free advice on all aspects of natural death and funerals. Contact the NDC: naturaldeath.org, phone 01962 712 690

Ch. 6

Different Funerals

As Great Britain is a multi-racial society, obviously not all funeral and burials are Christian burials. Some space must be given in a book like this to cover other funerals as they relate to different beliefs.

Muslim funerals

There are specific codes governing Muslim funerals. Normally, Muslims will appoint one person to represent them in deciding arrangements for funerals. Muslims are always buried and never cremated. There is usually no coffin, and the body is wrapped in a white sheet and buried within 24 hours of death in an unmarked grave, which must be raised up to 12 inches from the ground and can never be sat or walked upon.

Because of differences between the British tradition and Muslim requirements, one key difference being that a coffin is required in British cemeteries, special areas are sometimes designated by churches and other cemeteries. Because of the need to bury quickly, any requests for post-mortem or organ donation are usually refused, although a post-mortem will be necessary in the cases of suspicious deaths.

Muslims believe that the soul remains in the body sometime after death, and that the body remains conscious of pain. Bodies are therefore handled with care. Non-Muslims never handle bodies. Embalming is only usually allowed if a body is travelling over a long distance. The family will usually lay out a body and will place a head so that it is facing Mecca. Muslims must be buried facing Mecca. The family will normally perform all rites and blessings, together with the imam, the spiritual leader of the local mosque.

Hindu funerals

There are many Hindu deities, the three main ones being Brahma, the creator, Vishnu, the Preserver and Shiva, the Destroyer. Hindu belief in reincarnation means that most individuals face death in the hope of achieving a better life next time. Death is therefore relatively insignificant by comparison. Hindus are always cremated and never buried. Most Hindus bring their dead into a chapel of rest and candles are lit. There are not normally objections to the body being handled by non-Hindu, although there can be many variations on the theme because of the diversity of the religion. The Asian Funeral Service arranges Hindu funerals and organises repatriation for those who require a funeral by the Ganges.

Sikh funerals

Sikhism has a lot in common with Hinduism but there is a strong emphasis on militarism. There are five symbols of faith important to the Sikh. The Kesh is the uncut hair, which, for men, is always turbaned. The Kangha is a ritual comb, which keeps the hair in place and is never removed. The Kara is a steel bracelet worn on the right wrist. The Kirpan is a small symbolic dagger. The Kaccha are ceremonial undergarments, which are never completely removed even when bathing.

Sikhs are always cremated and never buried. The family will always insist that their dead are buried with all five K symbols.

After a death, men are dressed in a white cotton shroud and turban, older women in white and young women in red. Cremation will usually take place within 24 hours. The coffin will usually be taken home before cremation for last respects to be paid. The oldest son will press the crematoria button or see the coffin into the cremator. Ashes are scattered in a river or in the sea or taken back for scattering in the Punjab in India.

Buddhist funerals-Buddhist beliefs about death

Buddhists acknowledge death as a part of the cycle of reincarnation known as samsāra. In samsāra, a Buddhist's actions in life will affect future incarnations. Although widely accepted among Buddhists, this belief may differ slightly according to the type of Buddhism. Buddhists aspire to leave the cycle of samsāra by freeing themselves from all desires and notions of self to attain enlightenment and reach a state of nirvana.

Buddhist cremation

Many Buddhists prefer cremation to burial. Traditionally, Buddhist cremation may take place on an open-air pyre, but as this is prohibited in the UK, most Buddhists choose a cremation service at a local crematorium. The cremation ashes may be scattered, buried, or kept at home in an urn.

In some Buddhist cultures, such as in Japan, the family may want to watch the cremation process take place. This may be possible at your local crematorium – ask your funeral director if this can be arranged. However, burial is not unheard of in Buddhist funerals. Some Buddhists may opt for a woodland burial, as an environmentally friendly way to return to the earth.

Buddhist funeral traditions

Organ and body donation for transplant and research purposes are acceptable within Buddhism. Embalming is generally not encouraged, unless it is completely necessary, or the individual expressed a wish to be embalmed.

Buddhist funeral services

Normally Buddhist funerals are simple and dignified and take place at a Buddhist monastery or at a family home. The number of mourners expected can vary, often depending on the size of the venue.

There is no prescribed procedure that Buddhist funerals follow, so the funeral service may occur before cremation, after cremation or before burial. Depending on the arrangements, there may be an open coffin at the funeral service.

On arrival, mourners may be seeing an altar decorated with an image of the person who has died, an image of Buddha, flowers, incense, candles, and fruits. Mourners often present the bereaved with flowers, usually placed alongside their loved one or the decorated altar. Once all the mourners have paid their respects, monks and other members of the Buddhist community will read sermons and deliver eulogies. Chanting by monks regularly features in Buddhist funeral services, although the recordings of chants are sometimes played on these occasions instead.

Non-religious rites may be performed alongside those of Buddhism, if they do not conflict with Buddhist funeral rites and beliefs.

*

After a Buddhist funeral

Buddhism is a very diverse religion, existing in many different cultures. Whether or not there is a reception after the funeral may depend on the traditions of the family. Usually, if there is a reception, mourners will be invited to attend to pay their respects. Traditionally, Buddhist memorial services are held on the 3rd, 7th, 49th and 100th day after death. These dates, however, can be changed at the family's discretion.

Jewish funerals

Orthodox Jews are very strict when it comes to funerals while more progressive Jews have differing attitudes. When a Jewish person dies, the body is traditionally left for eight minutes while a feather is placed in the mouth or nostrils to detect signs of breathing. Eyes and mouth are then closed by the eldest son, or the nearest relative. Many Jews appoint "watchers" this being a person or people who will stay with the body day or night until the funeral, praying and reciting.

The dead are buried as soon as possible. Cremation is not accepted by the Orthodox Jew. Orthodox Rabbis will sometimes permit the burial of cremated remains in a full-size coffin and say Kaddish (prayer) for the deceased. Jewish funerals are usually arranged by a Jewish funeral agency. Otherwise, the local Jewish community will arrange a contract with a gentile Funeral Director, but under strict Rabbinical control. The Raphael Jewish Counselling Service offers support to those who have lost another raphaeljewishcounselling.org. 0800 234 6236.

Cult funerals

There are an enormous number of different cults in the U.K., including Mormons and Jehovah's Witnesses, Christian Scientists, Scientologists, Moonies, and the Children of God. For most there is little or no deviation from orthodox Christian practice. Some groups became prominent in the 1960's, such as Hare Krishna and will normally adopt Hindu practices.

****

Ch. 7

After a Funeral is over

Traditional funerals

When a funeral service is finished, there is usually a gathering of family and friends at the house of the deceased, or at a venue organized by relatives. The organising of this event is important, as mourners need to be clearly informed about what has been arranged and where it is being held.

(However, please consider the updated requirements of COVID 19 regulations by referring to the government website)

The funeral director (If used, depending on the funeral) will submit an account, which is usually very detailed and will require payment within a reasonable amount of time. If the money is from the estate, there should be no problem arranging for the release of the funds to pay for a funeral. Legally, payment of the funeral bill is the first claim on the estate of the deceased, taking priority over income tax and any other claims.

Memorials

As previously discussed, relatives of the deceased often want to place a memorial tablet or headstone in a churchyard or cemetery where the person is buried. There are normally restrictions on the size of the memorial and full details of the restrictions can be obtained from the burial ground. The funeral director or monumental mason will normally apply to the church or cemetery authorities for permission to erect a memorial. After a burial, several months should be allowed for settlement before any memorial is erected or replaced. Time and consideration should be given to a memorial, and names of Burial Authorities. The cost of memorial will vary enormously, depending on what has been purchased and a written estimate should be obtained before any order is given.

After cremation

About one week after cremation has taken place, the crematorium will usually send a brochure to the next of kin explaining what kinds of memorials are available. These are all optional and are not covered by the fees paid for the cremation.

The most popular means of memorial at the cremation is the book of remembrance. Hand lettered inscriptions in the book usually consist of the name, date of death, and a short epitaph. The charge depends on the length of entry. The crematorium displays the book, open at the right page, on the anniversary of the funeral.

The crematoria will provide a list of charges on request. Some crematoria have a colonnade of niches for ashes called a columbarium. The ashes are either walled in by a plaque or left in an urn by the niche. Charges for this are high, where space can be found. In addition to the above, some crematoria have memorial trees, or rose bushes. These are usually arranged in beds, where the memorial bush is chosen by the family, the ashes are scattered around it, and a small plaque placed nearby. Costs vary and can be provided by the crematoria in question.

Ashes generally

Once a cremation is over, if you want you can get the ashes back. There are several things that you can do with the ashes. You can bury them in your local cemetery or in a natural burial ground. You can scatter them. You can divide them up amongst members of the family. You can get the crematorium to scatter them. There are many things that can be done with the ashes. Here are a few suggestions:

- Keep the ashes in an urn, this is a very common way of dealing with the ashes

- Mix them in clay or some other material and make something with them
- Scatter them from a hot air balloon or aircraft
- Scatter them at sea
- Have them turned into a diamond-go to phoenix-diamonds.com
- Have them mixed with glass and made into an ornament or pendant. Go to ashesintoglass.co.uk
- Keep them in a locket, ring, or pendant. Go to urns-coffins-caskets.co.uk
- Have them made into a firework display. Go to heavensabovefireworks.com
- Fire them into space. Go to heavensabovefireworks.com

These are just a few options for you to think about.

Charitable donations

An increasing number of people will request that family and friends make a charitable donation to a nominated charity in memory of the deceased and will regard this as a fitting memorial for the person concerned. Usually, the funeral director will arrange to collect and forward donations and will not charge for this service.

****

Chapter 8

The Estate of the Deceased
Applying for Probate England and Wales,
Scotland and Northern Ireland

Applying for the legal right to deal with someone's property, money, and possessions (their 'estate') when they die is called 'applying for probate'. If the person left a will, you'll get a 'grant of probate'. If the person did not leave a will, you'll get 'letters of administration'. The process is different in Scotland and Northern Ireland that is discussed further on.

When probate is not needed
You may not need probate if the person who died:
- had jointly owned land, property, shares, or money - these will automatically pass to the surviving owners
- only had savings or premium bonds

Contact each asset holder (for example a bank or mortgage company) to find out if you'll need probate to get access to their assets. Every organisation has its own rules.

Who can apply?

Only certain people can apply for probate to deal with the estate of someone who died. It depends on whether the person who died left a will.

If there's a will

You can apply for probate if you're named in the will, or in an update to the will (a 'codicil'), as an 'executor'. If you do not want to apply for probate and there are no other named executors, contact your local probate office to find out what to do. You'll need the original will and any updates to apply for probate. These must be original documents, not photocopies.

If the person did not leave a will

It's the 'administrator' who deals with the estate. You can apply to become the estate's administrator if you were the deceased's:

- spouse (husband or wife) - even if you were separated
- civil partner
- child

You'll receive 'letters of administration' to prove you have the legal right to deal with the estate. You cannot apply if you're the partner of the person but were not their spouse or civil partner when they died. You're not automatically entitled to any of their estate unless you're able to make changes to the inheritance.

Work out who inherits

The law decides who inherits the estate if there's no will. You'll need this information to report the estate's value and find out if there's Inheritance tax due. If there's a dispute, you can challenge an application for probate ('enter a caveat') before it's granted.

If you're an executor

An executor is someone named in a will as responsible for sorting out the estate of the person who's died. The person who died will normally have told you if you're an executor. You'll need the original will to apply for probate.

Find the original will

The person who died should have told all the executors where to find the original will and any updates, for example:

- at their house
- with a solicitor
- at the London Probate Department - you'll need the death certificate and evidence you're the executor

If you cannot find the original will, you'll need to fill in a lost will form. If there's more than one will, only the most recent will is valid. Do not destroy any copies of earlier wills until you've received probate. An executor only receives assets if they're also named as a beneficiary.

If there's more than one executor

If more than one person is named as an executor, you must all agree who makes the application for probate. Up to 4 executors can be named on the application. If only one executor is named on the application, they'll need to prove that they tried to contact all executors named in the will before they applied. You can contact your local probate registry if you're having problems finding other executors. A probate registry cannot help with disagreements between executors. You'll need to find another way to reach an agreement - this could mean getting legal advice.

If you do not want to or cannot be an executor

The will may name a replacement executor for someone who becomes 'unwilling or unable' to deal with the estate. You should check if no executors are willing or able to apply for probate. If an executor wishes to step down then they would fill in form PA15, form of renunciation.

Before you apply

Check if you need probate, You must estimate and report the estate's value before you apply for probate. Depending on its value, you may have to pay Inheritance Tax.

If there's tax to pay, you normally must pay at least some of it before you'll get probate. You can claim the tax back from the estate or the beneficiaries if you pay it out of your own bank account. You cannot apply for probate until you have a notice from HM Revenue and Customs (HMRC) saying that you've either paid inheritance tax or have no tax to pay.

Probate application fees

The application fee is £273 (2022) if the value of the estate is £5,000 or over. There's no fee if the estate is under £5,000. Extra copies of the probate cost £1.50 each. This means you can send them to different organisations at the same time.

Get help and advice

If you've not yet applied and have a question about applying for probate, go to: www.gov.uk/applying-for-probate.

Apply for probate online

You can use this service, more commonly used during COVID, if you're the executor or administrator and you:

- have the original will if you're the executor (you do not need the will if you're an administrator)
- have the original death certificate or an interim death certificate from the coroner
- have already reported the estate's value

The person who died must have lived in England or Wales most of the time. The probate registry will keep the original will. If you make a copy of it for your records, do not remove any staples or bindings from the original.

Apply for probate by post
The form you need to fill in depends on whether the person left a will or not.

Fill in application form PA1P if there is a will.
Fill in application form PA1A if there is not a will.

At the time of writing, because of coronavirus (COVID-19), it's taking longer to process paper applications than online applications. Use the online service to apply for probate if you can. You need to pay before you send the form.

You can pay by either:

- calling the card payment phone number of your district probate registry between 9:30am and 3pm to pay by debit or credit card - you'll be given a reference number to send with your documents
- sending a cheque payable to HM Courts and Tribunals Service with your documents

Send your completed form to HMCTS Probate with the following documents:

- the original will and any additions to it ('codicils')
- 2 copies of the will and additions on plain A4 paper - do not remove any staples or bindings to make the copies
- the death certificate or an interim death certificate from the coroner

HMCTS Probate
PO Box 12625
Harlow
CM20 9QE

Use a signed-for or tracked postal service that will deliver to PO boxes to send your documents. The death certificate will be returned to you but the will and any updates to it will not be.

If the will has been changed or damaged

You must include a cover letter if the will or any updates have changed in any way since you've had them. This includes them being damaged or separated for photocopying. The letter should explain what's been changed and why.

After you've applied

You'll usually get the grant of probate (or letters of administration) within 4 weeks of sending in your original documents. However, it may take longer. You should not make any financial plans or put property on the market until you have received the grant or letters. Because of coronavirus (COVID-19), probate applications are taking between 4 and 8 weeks to process. If there's anything wrong with the grant of probate (or letters of administration), return it to the district probate registry listed on the grant or letters.

Send a copy to organisations that hold the assets of the person who died, for example their bank. Once you have probate you can start dealing with the estate.

Probate in Scotland

Dealing with a Deceased's Estate in Scotland-Applying for confirmation. When dealing with a deceased's estate, you may have been told that you need to obtain 'confirmation' before any money and other property, belonging to the deceased, can be released. It is often a bank, building society or insurance company that will ask for this. 'Confirmation' is a legal document from the court giving the executor(s) authority to uplift any money or other property belonging to a deceased person from the holder (such as the bank), and to administer and distribute it according to law. An application is lodged with the sheriff court.

This is only one part of the process in dealing with a deceased's estate, and is the part that the court is involved in. You will find some useful information on other parts of the process in the document 'What to do after a death in Scotland......practical advice for times of bereavement' produced by the Scottish Government.

When applying for confirmation, an executor must provide a list of all the deceased's property at the time of death. The list - called an inventory - might include money, houses, land and shares. Confirmation is possible only if the inventory includes at least one item of money or other property in Scotland.

Small Estate or Large Estate

There are two types of confirmation, for small estates and for large estates. A 'small estate' is an estate where the total value of the deceased's money and property is £36000 or less. A 'large estate' is an estate where the total value is above this. In calculating the total value, you should not deduct any debts, such as funeral expenses, gas or electricity bills, balance of mortgage, owed by the deceased. The values of bank accounts must also include interest to date of death.

The procedure, forms and fees are different depending on what type of estate the application relates to. If the estate is a small estate, then the sheriff clerk will be able to help you prepare the 'inventory', and you can contact your local sheriff court to arrange an appointment. If the estate is a large estate, it is advisable to seek legal advice. The Law Society of Scotland can provide contact details for solicitors in your area.

Presence of a will

The procedures are also different depending on whether the deceased left a will. If they did not leave a will, you might hear the estate being referred to as 'intestate'; if they did leave a will, you might hear the estate being referred to as 'testate'. If there was a will left and it complies with all the legal requirements in Scotland, then the information noted above in relation to small and large estates will apply. If they did not leave a will, then you may have to get a bond of caution before you apply for confirmation of the estate, further information on this can be received from the sheriff clerk. If it is a large estate, and there is no will, there is an additional step in the procedure. You would need to apply to be appointed executor, using the dative petition procedure.

Applications after confirmation has been issued:

Where the original executor has died or has become incapacitated without fully administering the estate of the deceased (Ad non executa); or

■ where additional estate is discovered or where estate has been wrongly valued in the original confirmation and the principal executors appointed will not or cannot act (Ad omissa).

The form to be used is Form X-1 Confirmation ad non executa / ad omissa

An application can also be made to court where an asset was not included in the original inventory. To do this, you would need to complete a corrective inventory and the form to be used is Form C4(S). Further information can be accessed on the HMRC website.

How much will it cost?

The fees for applying for confirmation will depend on the value of the estate and the number of certificates you need to provide for different banks, insurance companies etc. to allow them to release the funds. The current fees can be accessed in the Sheriff Court Fees section of the website.

You should note that these fees do not include any fees you may need to pay if you have instructed a solicitor to help you. The solicitor can give you information on these costs.

You cannot apply for fee exemption when applying for confirmation unless the estate of the deceased person is exempt from inheritance tax by virtue of:

- section 153A (death of emergency service personnel etc.),
- section 154 (death in active service etc.), or
- section 155A (death of constables and service personnel targeted because of their status)
- The Inheritance Tax Act 1984, in which case there is no fee in respect of the inventory of that estate. However, fees for certificates, copies, etc. remain payable in these circumstances.

Applying for probate in Northern Ireland

In Northern Ireland, a grant is almost always needed when the person who died leaves one or more of the following:

- £10,000 or more
- stocks or shares

- certain insurance policies
- property or land held in their own name or as 'tenants in common'

In most cases above, the bank or relevant institution will need to see the grant before transferring control of the assets. However, if the estate is small some organisations, such as insurance companies and building societies, may choose to release the money to you. You may not need a grant if the deceased:

- left less than £10,000
- owned everything jointly with someone else and everything passes automatically to the surviving joint owner
- To find out if the assets can be obtained without a grant, the executor or administrator would need to write to each institution informing them of the death and enclosing a photocopy of the death certificate and will if there is one.

Inheritance tax
You'll need to deal with inheritance tax before you can apply for probate.

Applying for a grant

You can apply for a grant without using a solicitor if the deceased was living in Northern Ireland and:

- left a valid Will and you are named as executor in that Will
- did not leave a Will but you are next of kin and are resident in the UK

To get a grant, you'll need to go to an interview bringing the required original documents with you, confirm the details in your application and sign the probate forms.

Probate fees

The fees to be paid are based on the net value of the estate and are made up of two parts, the grant fee, and the personal application fee.

Net value of the estate	Grant fee	Personal application fee
less than £10,000	nil	nil
more than £10,000	£261.00	£61.00

The personal application fee is only charged if you are applying for a grant without a solicitor. Certified copies of a grant cost £6.00 each. These are useful if you must deal with several financial institutions. For more information about Probate in Northern Ireland go to:

www.nidirect.gov.uk/articles/probate.

****

Ch. 9

The Intervention of the Courts

Introduction

Where an individual has died without making proper provision in their Will for their relatives or dependants, judges have a wide discretion to redistribute assets to produce a fair result.

Who can apply for an order?

Under the Inheritance (Provision for Family and Dependants) Act 1975 only certain people are entitled to make an application to the court for an order. Broadly speaking, these are the immediate family of the deceased, or their partner if they were living together as husband and wife (or as civil partners).

To make an application under the Inheritance Act, the applicant must also show that the deceased was 'domiciled' in England or Wales, which, in very broad terms, means that they were permanently based in this jurisdiction.

When to apply for an order

Any application under the Inheritance Act must be made within six months of the Personal Representatives obtaining a grant of probate to allow them to administer the estate. Outside this time limit, the court's permission will be needed to allow the applicant to begin proceedings. This permission is usually given only in exceptional circumstances.

Grounds for making a claim

There is only one ground for a claim under the Inheritance Act, which is that the disposition (or division) of the deceased's estate, whether following his Will or under the laws of Intestacy, does not make reasonable financial provision for the applicant.

Where the applicant is a spouse, or a civil partner, of the deceased, 'reasonable financial provision' means such provision as would be reasonable in all the circumstances of the case for a husband or wife or a civil partner to receive, whether that provision is required for his or her maintenance. The court must consider, but is not bound to follow, the likely settlement that would have made within divorce proceedings, if the parties had divorced rather than the deceased having died. You may hear this referred to as the 'divorce fiction'. For all other applicants under the Inheritance Act, 'reasonable financial provision' means such provision as it would be reasonable in all the circumstance of the case for the applicant to receive for his maintenance. Thus, the court will not make an order in these circumstances only because the applicant feels that the Will or Intestacy is unfair or is not as they expected. The applicant must show that he had a reasonable expectation of having his living costs met by the deceased. If the applicant was financially independent of the deceased before the date of death, it may be very difficult to show such an expectation.

Orders the court can make

The judge has a wide discretion to redistribute assets to provide a fair result. The court can make any of the following orders: -

a) an order that the applicant should receive regular payments (known as 'periodical payments') from the net estate of the deceased, for as much and for as long as the judge considers reasonable.

b) an order that the applicant should receive a single lump sum payment from the estate.

c) an order that a property owned by the deceased be transferred to the applicant.

d) an order for the settlement of any property for the benefit of the applicant i.e. an order creating a trust for the applicant

e) an order for the purchase of property using assets of the

125

estate, and for such property either to be transferred to the applicant or to be held in trust for his benefit. f) an order varying any pre- or post-nuptial (or pre- or post-civil partnership) settlement to which the deceased was a party, for the benefit of a surviving spouse or civil partner, or for a child or step-child of the deceased.

In cases where the court is satisfied that the applicant is in immediate need of financial assistance, but it is not yet possible to reach a final decision about the order that should be made, and the court is satisfied that there are assets available to meet the applicant's immediate needs, the court also has jurisdiction to make 'interim' orders for a payment or payments from the estate. Any such payments may be considered when a final order is made.

Factors The Court Must Consider

In deciding whether to make an order under the Inheritance Act, the court must first decide whether the Will of the deceased, or the laws of Intestacy, makes reasonable financial provision for the applicant, and only if such provision has not been made, whether and in what manner it should exercise its powers to make one of the above orders. The specific factors that the court must by law consider when deciding these questions are as follows: -

- the financial resources and financial needs which the applicant has or is likely to have in the foreseeable future.

- the financial resources and financial needs which any other applicant for an order under the Inheritance Act from the estate of the deceased has or is likely to have in the foreseeable future.

- the financial resources and financial needs which any beneficiary of the estate of the deceased has or is likely to have in the foreseeable future.

- any obligations and responsibilities which the deceased had towards any applicant for an order or towards any beneficiary of his estate.

- the size and nature of the net estate of the deceased

- any physical or mental disability of any applicant or any beneficiary of the estate

- any other matter, including the conduct of the applicant or any other person, which in the circumstances of the case the court may consider relevant.

In cases where the applicant is a spouse or civil partner, the court must also consider those factors given weight within divorce proceedings, such as the length of the marriage, or civil partnership, the contributions made by the parties to the family's welfare and the age of the applicant.

In cases where the applicant is a child or stepchild of the deceased, the court will also consider the way the applicant is being, or is expected to be, educated or trained. With stepchildren, the court will further look at the extent to which the deceased had taken on responsibility for the child's maintenance, whether any other person had a duty to maintain the child and whether the deceased, in taking responsibility for the child, was aware that she/he was not the natural parent. In cases where a claim is brought by a person being maintained by the deceased at the time of his death, the court will look at the extent to which, and the basis upon which, the deceased began maintaining the applicant and the length of time for which he had done so.

The Procedure

The procedure for Inheritance Act applications is governed by the Civil Procedure Rules. These are designed to assist litigants and to ensure that all cases are run as efficiently as possible, without incurring unnecessary legal costs. However, before issuing any application, your solicitor will wish to discuss with you the possibility of using a process of out of court Dispute Resolution (DR). This may involve mediation or 'round table' negotiations and is intended to assist the parties to reach a fair compromise, without involving the courts. Only if DR is inappropriate to your case, or is unsuccessful in settling your claim, will your solicitor advise you to issue court proceedings.

If you decide to issue proceedings, a claim form will be sent to the court, along with supporting documents where appropriate. These give details to the court of the basis of your application. Once issued, the claim and any supporting documentation will be served upon the defendants. The court will normally list a preliminary hearing, at which several directions may be given. These may include permission to the parties to file any evidence upon which they wish to rely, and orders to disclose any information or documents in their possession which may be relevant to the proceedings. The defendants will usually be given the opportunity to set out their arguments against your claim in a written 'Defence'.

Once all these documents have been filed, the court may list a further hearing, which is an opportunity for the judge and the parties to check that all directions have been complied with, all relevant information has been provided, and to set a timetable to move the case forward. The exact procedure for this stage of your case will vary depending upon the details of your claim, and your solicitor will advise you about this in more detail as appropriate. It is essential that you abide by any timetable or deadlines given by the court, as failure to do so may be prejudicial to your case.

There is an ongoing duty upon the parties to continue to negotiate even after proceedings have been issued. Failure to do so may be reflected in the eventual order in relation to costs if the matter proceeds to final hearing. If the parties have failed to reach an agreement, and once the court is satisfied that all necessary information is available, the matter will be listed for final hearing. At this hearing, the judge will normally want all parties to give evidence and may also want to hear evidence from any expert witnesses involved. After hearing this evidence, the judge will decide whether to make an order as outlined above.

Legal costs

Any agreement reached on financial provision should also provide for the payment of each party's legal costs. It is common for each party's costs to be met from the estate of the deceased if agreement is reached, although this is not always the case. If the matter proceeds to a final hearing, then the judge will decide, after making the final orders, what orders for costs to make. This could mean that each party pays their own costs, or one party pays the other's.

****

Ch.10

Welfare Benefits after Bereavement

In this chapter, we will also discuss the Government's Tell Us Once Service, for terminating benefits and all other government related documents, such as driving licenses and passports, and blue badges.

Bereavement benefits if you were married or in a civil partnership

Bereavement benefits are for people whose husband, wife or civil partner has died. Which benefits and how much you qualify for will depend on:

- Your age
- Whether you have dependent children
- Whether the person who died paid enough National Insurance Contributions during their working lives.

Bereavement Support Payment

If your spouse or civil partner died on or after 6 April 2017, you might be eligible to get Bereavement Support Payment to help you cope financially. The benefit is paid to you at one of two rates depending on whether you are responsible for children. You must be below State Pension Age to claim Bereavement Support Payment. Your spouse or civil partner must have made enough National Insurance Contributions during their working life for you to qualify. Bereavement Support Payment is only paid for 18 months after the date when your spouse or civil partner died so it's important you claim as soon as possible to avoid losing money.

How much is Bereavement Support Payment?

Bereavement Support Payment is paid at either a higher rate or standard rate:

Higher rate

Paid to pregnant women or if you're entitled to Child Benefit. You'll get:

- A monthly payment of £350 for 18 months following the death.
- A one-off payment of £3,500 during the first month.

Standard rate

For everyone else. You'll get:

- A monthly payment of £100 for 18 months.
- A one-off payment of £2,500 during the first month.

You might also be eligible to claim other low-income benefits to top up your income, like tax credits, Housing Benefit, Council Tax Reduction or Universal Credit.

How do I claim Bereavement Support Payment?

You can claim from the date when the person dies. Claims can be backdated up to three months only. So, make sure you make your claim within three months of your spouse or civil partner's death or you might lose some of your payments. Call the Bereavement Service helpline or pick up a form at your local JobCentre Plus.

Helpline

Bereavement Service helpline
Telephone: 0800 731 0469
Welsh language: 0800 731 0453
Textphone: 0800 731 0464

Bereavement benefits if you were living together

You can't claim bereavement benefits if you were living together but weren't married or in a civil partnership.

But you can try applying for other benefits, such as:

- Income Support
- Housing Benefit
- Universal credit, or
- Working Tax Credit

How to claim benefits if you're on a low income

If you're facing a drop in income after your partner dies, you might be able to claim a range of benefits to top up your income and help with things like housing costs or bringing up children. Some benefits are means-tested. This means any savings or income you have will affect whether you are entitled to benefit payments. This includes an inheritance taking your savings over the £16,000 threshold. Try to report the death as soon as you can. This will help you get the benefits you're entitled to as quickly as possible. To do this, you'll need to let the Department for Work and Pensions (DWP) know the person has died.

Funeral Payment

If you're on a low income and struggling to pay for a funeral for your partner, you can apply for a Funeral Payment. If the person who died left money, you will usually need to pay back any amount you received through the Funeral Payments scheme.

How much you will get

The amount you get depends on your circumstances but could be up to £700 towards funeral expenses plus payments to cover the costs of things like burial or cremation fees.

How your bereavement benefits affect other benefits

If you claim any of the following benefits, your payments might be affected if you start getting Bereavement Support Payment or are getting Bereavement Allowance or Widowed Parent's Allowance.

- Universal Credit
- Income Support
- Incapacity Benefit
- Jobseeker's Allowance
- Carer's Allowance
- Employment and Support Allowance
- Pension Credit (only if you receive Bereavement Allowance)

Bereavement Payment or the lump sum you get as part of Bereavement Support Payment counts as savings when your entitlement to some means-tested benefits is worked out. This means if you get the one-off lump sum payment, you might see a reduction in the following benefits:

- Income Support
- Housing Benefit
- Income-based Jobseeker's Allowance
- Employment and Support Allowance
- Universal Credit

To find out more about how other benefits might be affected, contact the Bereavement Service, which is run by the Pension Service of the Department of Work and Pensions (DWP):

If you live in England and Wales, call 0345 606 0265).

For the Welsh language helpline, call 0345 606 0275).

If you live in Northern Ireland, call 0800 085 2463 (free to call).

Benefits calculators

There are several benefit calculators which can help you work out what you're entitled to. For a general idea of the benefits you might be eligible for, use the Citizens Advice benefit calculator. For a more detailed breakdown of what you might get, use the Turn2us benefit calculator, or the Entitled to benefit calculator .

Tax and National Insurance

Your income will probably change after the death of your husband, wife, or civil partner. If you get extra money from pensions, annuities, benefits, or an inheritance, you may need to pay more tax. You may be on a lower income and need to pay less tax. Your tax allowances - the income you do not pay tax on - may also change.

Income you must report

Tell HMRC if you get:

- interest from a bank, building society or a National Savings and Investment product, eg pensioner income, capital bonds
- income from letting out property
- income from Purchased Life Annuities
- Widowed Parent's Allowance or Bereavement Allowance
- Carer's Allowance
- foreign pension payments
- other income that should have been taxed but has not been

You do not need to tell HMRC about:

- income your employer pays tax on through PAYE
- income from a private pension
- income which does not get taxed, e.g. from an Individual Savings Account (ISA)
- any income if you'll reach State Pension age within 4 months

■ getting Jobseeker's Allowance (JSA), Incapacity Benefit, Employment and Support Allowance (ESA) or Bereavement Support Payment

Tax allowances

If you pay Income Tax, you'll have a Personal Allowance - income you do not pay tax on. Your allowance may change if your income changes. HMRC will automatically adjust your Personal Allowance when you tell them about your change of income.

Married Couple's Allowance

If you or your husband, wife or civil partner were born before 6 April 1935, you may have been claiming Married Couple's Allowance. You'll still get the allowance for the current tax year (up to 5 April) but HMRC will automatically stop it after that and you'll get just your Personal Allowance.

Blind Person's Allowance

If your husband, wife or civil partner was claiming Blind Person's Allowance, ask HMRC to transfer what's left of their Blind Person's Allowance for the current tax year (up to 5 April) to you.

HMRC Blind Person's Allowance enquiries

Telephone: 0300 200 3301

Monday to Friday, 8am to 8pm

Saturday, 8am to 4pm

Reduced rate National Insurance

If you're a widow and you were married before April 1977, you might be paying a reduced rate of National Insurance (sometimes called the 'small stamp'). You may be able to keep paying the reduced rate. Contact HMRC to find out what you should do.

Pensions

You may be able to get extra pension payments from your husband, wife or civil partner's pension or National Insurance contributions.

State Pension

You need to be over State Pension age to claim extra payments from your husband, wife, or civil partner's State Pension. What you get and how you claim will depend on whether you reached State Pension age before or after 6 April 2016. Contact the Pension Service to check what you can claim. www.gov.uk/contact-pension-service. This site will also give guidance on the process in Scotland and Northern Ireland.

If you reached State Pension age before 6 April 2016

You'll get any State Pension based on your husband, wife, or civil partner's National Insurance contribution when you claim your own pension. You will not get it if you remarry or form a new civil partnership before you reach State Pension age.

If you reached State Pension age on or after 6 April 2016

You'll receive the 'new State Pension' and you may be able to inherit an extra payment on top of your pension.

Private pensions

You may get payments from your husband, wife or civil partner's workplace, personal or stakeholder pension - it will depend on the pension scheme. Contact the pension scheme to find out. You'll have to pay tax on those payments if the pension provider does not pay it for you.

War Widow's or Widower's Pension

You may be able to get War Widow's or Widower Pension - if your husband, wife, or civil partner died because of their service in the Armed Forces or because of a war.

*

Financial help if your husband, wife or civil partner was in the Armed Forces

If your husband, wife or civil partner died as a result of serving in the Armed Forces, you may be able to get financial help from Veterans UK 0808 1914 218. It does not matter whether your husband, wife or civil partner died during active service or not, if the death was caused by service in the Armed Forces. You may get a War Widow's or War Widower's pension, or a guaranteed income payment (based on your spouse or civil partner's earnings), depending on when the injury, illness or death was caused. You can get more information on guaranteed income payments, the war pension scheme, and the Armed Forces Compensation Scheme on GOV.UK.

The Tell Us Once Service

The very last thing that people who have lost a spouse or partner wants is to be wrestling with the different areas that need to be cancelled following death. To this end, the government has devised the Tell us Once Service, which streamlines the process.

If you live in England, Scotland, or Wales you can contact the Tell Us Once service to cancel the deceased's benefits and entitlements.

The Tell Us Once service is a government service, offered by most local authorities which also informs the DVLA, HMRC, Passport Office and local council for you and check if you're eligible for help with funeral costs or other benefits.

How to use Tell Us Once

A registrar will explain the Tell Us Once service when you register the death.

They will either:

- complete the Tell Us Once service with you
- give you a unique reference number so you can use the service yourself online or by phone

The registrar will give you a number to call. This includes a video relay service for British Sign Language (BSL) users and Relay UK if you cannot hear or speak on the phone.

You must use the service within 28 days of getting your unique reference number. If you cannot register the death because an inquest is underway, you can still ask a registrar for a unique reference number. You'll need to get an interim death certificate from the coroner holding the inquest first.

Before you use Tell Us Once

You'll need the Tell Us Once reference number that you got from the registrar. You'll also need the following details of the person who died:

- name
- date of birth
- address
- date they died
- name, address and contact details of the person or company dealing with their estate (property, belongings, and money), known as their 'executor' or 'administrator'
- if there's a surviving spouse or civil partner, the name, address, telephone number and the National Insurance number or date of birth of the spouse or civil partner
- if there's no surviving spouse or civil partner or their spouse or civil partner is not able to deal with their affairs, the name and address of their next of kin
- if they died in a hospital, nursing home, care home or hospice, the name and address of that institution - you'll also be asked if the stay was for 28 days or more

You may also need:

- if they had a passport, their passport number and town of birth

- if they had a driving licence, their driving licence number
- if they owned any vehicles, the vehicle registration numbers
- if they were getting services from their local council, such as Housing Benefit payments or Council Tax reductions, the name of their local council and which services they were getting
- if they were getting any benefits, tax credits or State Pension, information about which ones they were getting
- if they were getting money from an Armed Forces Pension or Compensation Scheme, details of that scheme
- if they were getting money or paying into public sector pension schemes, details of those schemes
- if they were getting money or paying into Local Government Pension Schemes (LGPS), details of those schemes and their National Insurance number
- Unless they were involved in a LGPS, you do not need their National Insurance number. If you can still provide it though, it will help some organisations match their records faster.

- You need permission from any surviving spouse or civil partner, the next of kin, executor, administrator, or anyone who was claiming joint benefits or entitlements with the person who died before you give their details.

Organisations Tell Us Once will contact

Tell Us Once will notify:

- HM Revenue and Customs (HMRC) - to deal with personal tax and to cancel benefits and credits, for example Child Benefit and tax credits (you need to contact HMRC separately for business taxes, like VAT)
- Department for Work and Pensions (DWP) - to cancel benefits and entitlements, for example Universal Credit or State Pension
- Passport Office - to cancel a British passport
- Driver and Vehicle Licensing Agency (DVLA) - to cancel a licence, remove the person as the keeper of up to 5 vehicles and end the vehicle tax (you must contact DVLA separately if you either sell the vehicle or keep it and tax it in your own name)
- the local council - to cancel Housing Benefit, Council Tax Reduction (sometimes called Council Tax Support),

a Blue Badge, inform council housing services and remove the person from the electoral register

- Veterans UK - to cancel or update Armed Forces Compensation Scheme payments
- Social Security Scotland - to cancel benefits and entitlements from the Scottish Government, for example Scottish Child Payment

HMRC and DWP will contact you about the tax, benefits and entitlements of the person who died.

Tell Us Once will also contact some public sector pension schemes so that they cancel future pension payments. They'll notify:

- My Civil Service Pension
- NHS Pensions for NHS staff in England and Wales
- Armed Forces Pension Scheme
- Scottish Public Pension Agency schemes for NHS staff, teachers, police, and firefighters in Scotland
- Local Government Pension Schemes (LGPS) that participate in Tell Us Once

If you do not use Tell Us Once
You must let the relevant organisations know about the death yourself if either:

- you choose not to use the Tell Us Once service
- you cannot use Tell Us Once because the person died when they were living abroad

Banks and other financial organisations

Contact the person's bank or mortgage, pension, or insurance providers to close or change the details of accounts.

Update property records when someone dies

Although not part of Tell us Once, it is very important to update property records when someone dies.

How you update the property records when someone dies depends on whether they were the joint or sole owner of a property.

Check the property records if you don't know:

- who owns a property?
- whether it's owned jointly or solely

When a joint owner dies

When a joint owner of a property dies, fill in form DJP to remove their name from the register. Send the completed form to HM Land Registry, along with an official copy of the death certificate.

When a sole owner dies

When the sole owner of a property has died, the property is normally transferred to either:

- the person inheriting the property (known as 'the beneficiary')
- a third party, for example someone buying the property

If you transfer to a beneficiary

- To transfer a property to a beneficiary, download and fill in the following forms:
- 'Change the register' (sometimes known as form AP1)
- 'Whole of registered title: assent' (sometimes known as form AS1)
- You must also send:
- the original or an official copy of the grant of probate or letters of administration
- the Stamp Duty Land Tax certificate or self-certificate, or Land Transaction Tax certificate for properties sold in Wales on or after 1 April 2018 (if tax was paid on the property)
- a fee – check the land registry for fees.

- beneficiary must fill in 'Verify identity: citizen' (sometimes known as form ID1). You'll also need to complete the form if you're transferring the property and you're not the executor.
- Send all the completed forms and supporting documents to HM Land Registry.

If you sell the property to a third party

You need to:

- transfer the ownership of the property
- provide the buyer with an official copy of the probate or letters of administration

****

Useful Addresses

There are several agencies that provide help to those who have experienced bereavement. Below is a list of the key agencies with addresses, phone numbers and in most cases e mails.

Age UK
England
Tavis House
1-6 Tavistock Square
London
WC1H 9NA
0800 055 6112
E mail contact: @ageuk.org.uk

Scotland
Causeway House
160 Causewayside
Edinburgh EH9 1PR
Tel: 0333 3232 400
info@agescotland.org.uk

Northern Ireland
3 Lower Crescent

Belfast BT7 1NR

0808 808 7575 8am-7am (365 days a year)

info@ageni.org

Wales

Age Cymru,

Ground Floor, Mariners House,

Trident Court,

East Moors Road,

Cardiff, CF24 5TD.

Tel: 029 2043 1555

www.ageuk.org.uk/cymru

Asian Funeral Service (Leicester Branch)

260 Loughborough Road

LE54 5LH

0116 319 8232

Cruse-Bereavement Care

PO Box 800

Richmond, TW9 1RG

Tel: 0808 808 1677

info@cruse.org.uk

Foundation for the Study of Infant Death (The Lullaby Trust)
11 Belgrave Road
London SW1V 1RB
Tel: 0207 802 3200
office@lullabytrust.org.uk

Funeral Planning Authority
Barham Court
Teston
Maidestone Kent
0345 601 9619 www.funeralplanning authority.com

Institute of Family Therapy
24-32 Stephenson Way
London NW1 2HX
Tel: 0207 391 9150
Fax: 0207 391 9169
www.ift.org.uk

Jewish Bereavement Counseling Service
c/o Maurice and Vivienne Wohl Campus
221 Golders Green Road
London NW11 9DQ
0208 922 2222
enquiries@jbcs.org.uk

National Association of Funeral Directors

618 Warwick Road

Solihull

West Midlands B91 1AA

0121 711 1343

www.nafd.org.uk

National Association of Memorial Masons

1 Castle Mews

Rugby, CV21 2XL

Tel: 01788 542 264

www.namm.org.uk

****

Index

After cremation, 5, 104
Asian Funeral Service, 96, 152

Benefits agency, 49
Brain donation, 39
Bringing the body home, 44
British Consulate, 42, 43, 46
Buddhist funerals, 5, 97
Burial in cemeteries, 4, 72
Burial in Scotland, 4, 90

Cemeteries, 73, 88
Certificate of cause of death, 3, 19
Charitable donations, 5, 106
Church of England, 4, 65, 66, 73, 79, 85, 88
Church of England Burial, 65
Cornea, 37
Coroner, 19, 21
Costs of a funeral, 4, 56
Council Tax Benefit, 67
Cremation, 4, 45, 75, 89, 97, 100
Cult funerals, 5, 101

Death Certificates, 42
Death in a hospital, 3, 29
Disability Working allowance, 67
Donation of a body for medical uses, 38
Donation of the brain for medical research, 3, 39

Embalming a body, 4, 84

Family Credit, 67
Family of the deceased, 21
Fees for cremation, 4, 77
Foreign and Commonwealth Office, 43, 46
Funeral costs, 45
Funeral director, 18, 53, 65

Green certificate, 23

Hare Krishna, 101
Heart, 36, 37
High Court, 21
Hindu funerals, 5, 89, 96
HM Inspector of Anatomy, 38
Housing benefit, 67
Hypostasis, 18

Income support, 67
Industrial disease, 20
Institute of Neurology, 39

Jewish funerals, 5, 100
Job seekers allowance, 67

Kidney, 36

Last offices, 17
Laying out, 3, 17, 83
Laying out a body, 3, 17
Liver, 36
London local Authorities Act 2007, 71
Lungs, 37

Memorials, 5, 104
Military service, 20
Ministry of Defence, 68
Muslim funerals, 5, 95

National Association of Funeral Directors, 154
National Association of pre-paid Funeral Plans, 54
National Health Service Organ Donor Register, 38
Non-Church of England Funerals, 85
Non-religious services, 4, 86

Order for Burial, 45
Organ transplants, 35
Orthodox Jews, 85, 100

Pancreas, 36
Parkinson' Disease Society Brain Research Centre, 39
Police custody, 20
Police involvement, 3, 18
Post-mortem, 21
Procurator Fiscal, 40

Registering a stillbirth, 3, 26
Registering death, 22
Registrar of Deaths, 40
Registration in Scotland, 3, 39
Registration of death, 3, 22
Remains, 4, 79
Rigor Mortis, 18
Roman Catholic, 73, 85, 88
Royal College of Surgeons, 35

Services in a crematorium, 4, 78

Sikhs, 5, 97
Social Fund Payment, 68
Society of Allied and Independent Funeral Directors, 54
Suicide, 20

Tell Us Once Service, 7, 141
The burial, 4, 71, 72, 85, 88
The Funeral Standards Council, 54
The National Association of Funeral Directors, 54
The National Health Service Organ Donor Register, 38
The Parkinson' Disease Society Brain Research Centre, 39
The Social Fund, 68
Types of grave, 4, 74

UK Transplant Support Service Authority (UKTSSA), 38

When someone dies abroad, 42
Woodland burial, 75

**